The Little Mongo DB Schema Design Book

Christian Kvalheim

The Little Mongo DB Schema Design Book

Christian Kvalheim

This book is for sale at http://leanpub.com/mongodbschemadesign

This version was published on 2015-10-09

Leanpub

This is a Leanpub book. Leanpub empowers authors and publishers with the Lean Publishing process. Lean Publishing is the act of publishing an in-progress ebook using lightweight tools and many iterations to get reader feedback, pivot until you have the right book and build traction once you do.

Tweet This Book!

Please help Christian Kvalheim by spreading the word about this book on Twitter!

The suggested hashtag for this book is #mongodbschema.

Find out what other people are saying about the book by clicking on this link to search for this hashtag on Twitter:

https://twitter.com/search?q=#mongodbschema

Contents

1. Introduction

One of the questions that comes up very often from new users of MongoDB and document databases is how to do schema design. The concepts of embedding and linking documents combined with many years of working with relational models means there is a learning process involved in moving to a document database.

As the product has matured over time, some patterns of schema design have emerged. This book is an attempt to distill that knowledge into actionable information you can use for your own applications.

We will cover basics of MongoDB schema design, how MongoDB works under the covers and look at a series of schema design patterns that aim to solve specific issues that you might run into while working on your application.

That said, this is not the end all of schema design for MongoDB. If you come up with other brilliant schema design patterns feel free to drop me an email at christkv@gmail.com or send me a tweet to @christkv

I hope you enjoy the book and find the information useful.

Christian Amor Kvalheim

2. Schema Basics

Before exploring the more advanced schemas in this book it's important to revisit schema basics. In this chapter we will explore the basic relationships from traditional relational databases and how they relate to the document model in MongoDB.

We will start with a look at the One-To-One (1:1) relationship then moving on to the One-To-Many (1:N) and finally the Many-To-Many (N:M).

3. One-To-One (1:1)

The *1:1* relationship describes a relationship between two entities. In this case the *Author* has a single *Address* relationship where an *Author* lives at a single *Address* and an *Address* only contains a single *Author*.

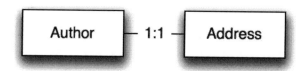

A One to One Relational Example

The *1:1* relationship can be modeled in two ways using MongoDB. The first is to embed the relationship as a document, the second is as a link to a document in a separate collection. Let's look at both ways of modeling the one to one relationship using the following two documents:

3.1 Model

An example User document

```
1  {
2    name: "Peter Wilkinson",
3    age: 27
4  }
```

An example Address document

```
1  {
2    street: "100 some road",
3    city: "Nevermore"
4  }
```

Embedding

The first approach is simply to embed the *Address* document as an embedded document in the *User* document.

An example User document with Embedded Address

```
1  {
2    name: "Peter Wilkinson",
3    age: 27,
4    address: {
5      street: "100 some road",
6      city: "Nevermore"
7    }
8  }
```

The strength of embedding the *Address* document directly in the *User* document is that we can retrieve the user and its addresses in a single read operation versus having to first read the user document and then the address documents for that specific user. Since addresses have a strong affinity to the user document the embedding makes sense here.

Linking

The second approach is to link the address and user document using a `foreign key`.

An example User document

```
1  {
2    _id: 1,
3    name: "Peter Wilkinson",
4    age: 27
5  }
```

An example Address document with Foreign Key

```
1  {
2    user_id: 1,
3    street: "100 some road",
4    city: "Nevermore"
5  }
```

This is similar to how traditional relational databases would store the data. It is important to note that MongoDB does not enforce any foreign key constraints so the relation only exists as part of the application level schema.

Embedding Preferred

In the one to one relationship Embedding is the preferred way to model the relationship as it's more efficient to retrieve the document.

4. One-To-Many (1:N)

The *1:N* relationship describes a relationship where one side can have more than one relationship while the reverse relationship can only be single sided. An example is a *Blog* where a blog might have many *Comments* but a *Comment* is only related to a single *Blog*.

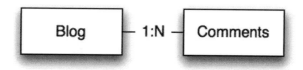

A One to Many Relational Example

The *1:N* relationship can be modeled in several different ways using MongoDB. In this chapter we will explore three different ways of modeling the *1:N* relationship. The first is embedding, the second is linking and the third is a bucketing strategy that is useful for cases like time series. Let's use the model of a Blog Post and its Comments.

4.1 Model

An example Blog Post document

```
1  {
2    title: "An awesome blog",
3    url: "http://awesomeblog.com",
4    text: "This is an awesome blog we have just started"
5  }
```

A Blog Post is a single document that describes one specific blog post.

Some example Comment documents

```
1  {
2    name: "Peter Critic",
3    created_on: ISODate("2014-01-01T10:01:22Z"),
4    comment: "Awesome blog post"
5  }
6
7  {
8    name: "John Page",
9    created_on: ISODate("2014-01-01T11:01:22Z"),
10   comment: "Not so awesome blog"
11 }
```

For each Blog Post we can have one or more Comments.

Embedding

The first approach is to embed the Comments in the Blog Post.

A Blog Post with Embedded documents

```
 1  {
 2    title: "An awesome blog",
 3    url: "http://awesomeblog.com",
 4    text: "This is an awesome blog we have just started",
 5    comments: [{
 6      name: "Peter Critic",
 7      created_on: ISODate("2014-01-01T10:01:22Z"),
 8      comment: "Awesome blog post"
 9    }, {
10      name: "John Page",
11      created_on: ISODate("2014-01-01T11:01:22Z"),
12      comment: "Not so awesome blog"
13    }]
14  }
```

The embedding of the comments in the *Blog* post means we can easily retrieve all the comments belong to a particular *Blog* post. Adding new comments is as simple as appending the new comment document to the end of the comments array.

However, there are three potential problems associated with this approach that one should be aware off.

- The first is that the comments array might grow larger than the maximum document size of 16 MB.
- The second aspects relates to write performance. As comments get added to Blog Post over time, it becomes hard for MongoDB to predict the correct document padding to apply when a new document is created. MongoDB would need to allocate new space for the growing document. In addition, it would have to copy the document to the new memory location and update all indexes. This could cause a lot more IO load and could impact overall write performance.

 It's important to note that this only matters for *high write* traffic and might not be a problem for smaller applications. What might not be acceptable for a *high write* volume application might be tolerable for an application with *low write* load.

- The third problem is exposed when one tries to perform pagination of the comments. There is no way to limit the comments returned from the Blog Post using normal finds so we will have to retrieve the whole blog document and filter the comments in our application.

Linking

The second approach is to link comments to the Blog Post using a more traditional foreign key.

An example Blog Post document

```
1   {
2     _id: 1,
3     title: "An awesome blog",
4     url: "http://awesomeblog.com",
5     text: "This is an awesome blog we have just started"
6   }
```

Some example Comment documents with Foreign Keys

```
1   {
2     blog_entry_id: 1,
3     name: "Peter Critic",
4     created_on: ISODate("2014-01-01T10:01:22Z"),
5     comment: "Awesome blog post"
6   }
7
8   {
9     blog_entry_id: 1,
10    name: "John Page",
11    created_on: ISODate("2014-01-01T11:01:22Z"),
12    comment: "Not so awesome blog"
13  }
```

An advantage this model has is that additional comments will not grow the original Blog Post document, making it less likely that the applications will run in the maximum document size of 16 MB. It's also much easier to return paginated comments as the application can slice and dice the comments more easily. On the downside if we have 1000 comments on a blog post, we would need to retrieve all 1000 documents causing a lot of reads from the database.

Bucketing

The third approach is a hybrid of the two above. Basically, it tries to balance the rigidity of the embedding strategy with the flexibility of the linking strategy. For this example, we will split the comments into buckets with a maximum of 50 comments in each bucket.

An example Blog Post document

```
1  {
2    _id: 1,
3    title: "An awesome blog",
4    url: "http://awesomeblog.com",
5    text: "This is an awesome blog we have just started"
6  }
```

Some example Comment buckets

```
1  {
2    blog_entry_id: 1,
3    page: 1,
4    count: 50,
5    comments: [{
6      name: "Peter Critic",
7      created_on: ISODate("2014-01-01T10:01:22Z"),
8      comment: "Awesome blog post"
9    }, ...]
10 }
11
12 {
13   blog_entry_id: 1,
14   page: 2,
15   count: 1,
16   comments: [{
17     name: "John Page",
```

```
18      created_on: ISODate("2014-01-01T11:01:22Z"),
19      comment: "Not so awesome blog"
20    }]
21  }
```

The main benefit of using buckets in this case is that we can perform a single read to fetch 50 comments at a time, allowing for efficient pagination.

 When to use bucketing

When you have the possibility of splitting up your documents into discreet batches, it makes sense to consider bucketing to speed up document retrieval.

Typical cases where bucketing is appropriate are ones such as bucketing data by hours, days or number of entries on a page (like comments pagination).

5. Many-To-Many (N:M)

An *N:M* relationship is an example of a relationship between two entities where they both might have many relationships between each other. An example might be a *Book* that was written by many *Authors*. At the same time an *Author* might have written many *Books*.

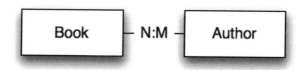

A Many to Many Relational Example

N:M relationships are modeled in the relational database by using a join table. A good example is the relationship between books and authors.

- An author might have authored multiple books (1:N).
- A book might have multiple authors (1:M).

This leads to an *N:M* relationship between authors of books. Let's look at how this can be modeled.

5.1 Two Way Embedding

Embedding the books in an Author document

Model

In Two Way Embedding we will include the *Book* foreign keys under the books field.

Some example Author documents

```
1    {
2      _id: 1,
3      name: "Peter Standford",
4      books: [1, 2]
5    }
6
7    {
8      _id: 2,
9      name: "Georg Peterson",
10     books: [2]
11   }
```

Mirroring the *Author* document, for each *Book* we include the *Author* foreign keys under the *Author* field.

Some example Book documents

```
1    {
2      _id: 1,
3      title: "A tale of two people",
4      categories: ["drama"],
5      authors: [1, 2]
6    }
7
8    {
9      _id: 2,
10     title: "A tale of two space ships",
11     categories: ["scifi"],
12     authors: [1]
13   }
```

Queries

Example 1: Fetch books by a specific author

```
1  var db = db.getSisterDB("library");
2  var booksCollection = db.books;
3  var authorsCollection = db.authors;
4
5  var author = authorsCollection.findOne({name: "Peter Standford"});
6  var books = booksCollection.find({_id: {$in: author.books}}).toArray();
```

Example 2: Fetch authors by a specific book

```
1  var db = db.getSisterDB("library");
2  var booksCollection = db.books;
3  var authorsCollection = db.authors;
4
5  var book = booksCollection.findOne({title: "A tale of two space ships"});
6  var authors = authorsCollection.find({_id: {$in: book.authors}}).toArray();
```

As can be seen, we have to perform two queries in both directions. The first is to find either the author or the book and the second is to perform a $in query to find the books or authors.

Uneven n:m relationships

Let's take the category `drama` that might have thousands of books in it and with many new books consistently being added and removed. This makes it impracticable to embed all the books in a category document. Each book, however, can easily have categories embedded within it, as the rate of change of categories for a specific book might be very low.

In this case we should consider `One way embedding` as a strategy.

5.2 One Way Embedding

The One Way Embedding strategy chooses to optimize the read performance of a *N:M* relationship by embedding the references in one side of the relationship. An example might be where several books belong to a few categories but a couple categories have many books. Letâ€™s look at an example, pulling the categories out into a separate document.

Model

A Category document

```
1  {
2    _id: 1,
3    name: "drama"
4  }
```

A Book with Foreign Keys for Categories

```
1  {
2    _id: 1,
3    title: "A tale of two people",
4    categories: [1],
5    authors: [1, 2]
6  }
```

The reason we choose to embed all the references to categories in the books is due to there being lot more books in the drama category than categories in a book. If one embeds the books in the category document it's easy to foresee that one could break the 16MB max document size for certain broad categories.

Queries

Example 3: Fetch categories for a specific book

```
1   var db = db.getSisterDB("library");
2   var booksCol = db.books;
3   var categoriesCol = db.categories;
4
5   var book = booksCol.findOne({title: "A tale of two space ships"});
6   var categories = categoriesCol.find({_id: {$in: book.categories}}).toArray();
```

Example 4: Fetch books for a specific category

```
1   var db = db.getSisterDB("library");
2   var booksCollection = db.books;
3   var categoriesCollection = db.categories;
4
5   var category = categoriesCollection.findOne({name: "drama"});
6   var books = booksCollection.find({categories: category.id}).toArray();
```

 Establish Relationship Balance

Establish the maximum size of N and the size of M. For example if N is a maximum of 3 categories for a book and M is a maximum of 500000 books in a category you should pick One Way Embedding. If N is a maximum of 3 and M is a maximum of 5 then Two Way Embedding might work well.

6. MMAP Storage Engine

The main storage engine in MongoDB is the Memory Mapped Storage Engine or MMAP for short. The MMAP storage engine uses memory mapped files as its storage engine.

6.1 Overview

- Uses memory mapped files to store data
- Allocates memory using power of 2 byte sizes (32, 64, 128, 256, ... 2MB)
- In place updates are fast
- Db level locking from MongoDB 2.2, Collection level locking from 3.0
- Benefits from preallocation strategy
- Can cause fragmentation
- No compression available (stores documents with all keys)

6.2 Memory Mapped Files

The MMAP Storage engine uses memory mapped files to store its data (A memory-mapped file is a segment of virtual memory which has been assigned a direct byte-for-byte correlation with some portion of a file).

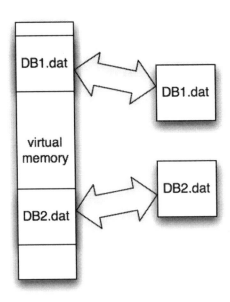

A General Example Of How Memory Mapped Files Work

Memory mapped files allow MongoDB to delegate the handling of Virtual Memory to the operating system instead of explicitly managing memory itself. Since the Virtual Address Space is much larger than any physical RAM (Random Access Memory) installed in a computer there is contention about what parts of the Virtual Memory is kept in RAM at any given point in time. When the operating system runs out of RAM and an application requests something that's not currently in RAM, it will swap out memory to disk to make space for the newly requested data. Most operating systems will do this using a Least Recently Used (LRU) strategy where the oldest data is swapped to disk first.

When reading up on MongoDB, you'll most likely run into the words "Working Set". This is the data that your application is constantly requesting. If your "Working Set" all fits in RAM, then all access will be fast because the operating system will not have to swap back and forth from disk as often. However, if your "Working Set" does not fit in RAM, you suffer performance penalties as the operating system needs to swap one part of your "Working Set" to disk, in order to access another part of it.

This is usually a sign that it's time to consider either increasing the amount of RAM in your machine or to shard your MongoDB system so more of your "Working Set" can be kept in memory (sharding splits your "Working Set" across multiple machines RAM resources).

Determine if the Working Set is too big

You can get an indication of if your working set fits in memory by looking at the number of page faults over time. If it's rapidly increasing it might mean your Working Set does not fit in memory.

```
use mydb
db.serverStatus().extra_info.page_faults
```

6.3 Allocation

From MongoDB 2.6 the default allocation method in MongoDB the power of two sized memory blocks. This means that it allocates blocks in the following byte sizes (32, 64, 128, 256, 512 ... up to 2MB).

Before 2.6 MongoDB would allocate blocks of memory that were the size of the document as well as some additional free space at the end of it to allow the document to grow. This was called the padding factor. Unfortunately there were several pathological MongoDB usage scenarios that could cause inefficient reuse of these allocated blocks slowly increasing fragmentation. A typical one was a heavy insert/update/delete cycle with random sized documents.

An example is below.

```
1   Documents inserted with different sizes
2
3       Doc 1: 24 bytes
4       Doc 2: 12 bytes
5
6   Documents are growing constantly requiring new allocations
7
8       Doc 1: 34 bytes, then 64 bytes, then 234 bytes
9       Doc 2: 450 bytes, then 1034, then 233 bytes
10
11  Documents are then removed from the database
12
13  As new documents are inserted the server cannot reuse the non uniform memory allocati\
14  ons.
15
16      Doc 3: 333 bytes requires new allocation
```

Over time this could cause memory allocations, which could not be reused by the server leading to memory fragmentation in the memory mapped files.

Fragmentation

When documents move around or are removed they leave holes. MongoDB tries to reuse these holes for new documents whenever possible, but over time it will slowly and steadily find itself having a lot of holes that cannot be reused because documents cannot fit into them. This effect is called fragmentation and is common in all systems that allocate memory including your operating system.

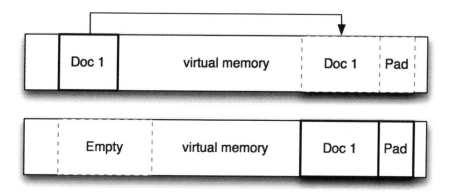

Document With Padding

The effect of fragmentation is to waste space. Due to the fact that MongoDB uses memory mapped files, any fragmentation will be reflected as fragmentation in RAM. This has the effect of reducing the "Working Set" that fits in RAM and causes more swapping to disk degrading performance.

How to determine the fragmentation

You can get a good indication of fragmentation by

```
use mydb
var s = db.my_collection.stats()
var frag = s.storageSize / (s.size + s.totalIndexSize)
```

A `frag` value larger than 1 indicates some level of fragmentation

There are three main ways of avoiding or limiting fragmentation for your MongoDB data.

The first one is to use the `compact` command on MongoDB to rewrite the data thus remove the fragmentation.

Power of 2 Allocation

Power of 2 allocations is a trade off between the higher likelihood of being able to reuse allocated blocks of memory, against potentially underutilization of those blocks.

Let's look at two examples, one optimal for power of 2 allocation and one that causes a lot of underutilized blocks of memory.

The first scenario

```
1   User writes document of 510 bytes
2   Each document fit nicely in a 512 bytes allocation slot
3   Only 2 bytes per document is left unused in an allocation slot
```

The second scenario

```
1   User writes document of 513 bytes
2   The document only fits in the 1024 byte allocation
3   For each document 510 bytes are left unused in the allocation slot
```

As we can see, there are some drastic edge cases. However, this is outweighed by the fact that documents which outgrow their allocation can easily be moved to a either a new allocation or an existing empty one of bigger size.

The Power of 2 allocations feature also reduces the level of fragmentation possible, as there is a bigger chance of allocation reuse than the previous method used in MongoDB.

Exact fit (no padding) allocation strategy (MongoDB 3.0)

MongoDB 3.0 introduces the possibility of using an exact fit allocation strategy. This disables the power of 2 allocation strategy and is useful if your workload is inserts only, with no updates or removals of the document. This can be enabled by using the server collMod command with the noPadding flag set to true or when creating a new collection using the createCollection command in the shell with the noPadding option set to true.

Preallocation strategy

Preallocation is a strategy to minimize the amount of times a document moves. It aims to avoid the situation where a document is moved in memory as it grows in size. Let's look at an example of the behavior we are trying to avoid.

```
1    Document 1 is written as a 123 byte document and put in a 128 byte allocation
2    Document 1 grows by 10 bytes and is copied to a 256 byte allocation
```

This can cause a lot of pointless work, requiring MongoDB to spend most of its time copying data causing the write and read performance to drop.

In many cases we might have documents that are in fact uniformly sized. Let's take the example of a time series where we are counting the number of times a web page is viewed.

```
1    {
2        , minute: {
3            "0": 1
4        }
5    }
```

When we register a measurement for a new second in the minute, the document gets another field added to the embedded document in the minute field.

```
1    {
2        , minute: {
3            "0": 1, "1": 1
4        }
5    }
```

But since we know there are only 60 entries in the minute embedded document we can ensure that it does not grow by preallocating an empty document that has the maximum size the document will be. So we can insert a full size document for each minute.

```
1    {
2        , minute: {
3            "0": 0, "1": 0, "2": 0....., "59": 0
4        }
5    }
```

This would avoid updates to the document growing it, This means all the updates would be in place ensuring the highest write performance the MMAP engine can provide.

6.4 Locking

MongoDB 2.6 introduced database level locking in 2.2 and improves on this in 3.0 with collection level locking. The lock references the write lock. When MongoDB only supported database level locking there could only be a single writer in a database. Let's look at an example.

```
1  Driver Writes Document 1 to database test
2  Driver Writes Document 2 to database test
```

When a write happens under database level locking no other reads or writes can happen concurrently until the first write finishes. In the example above Document 2 has to wait until Document 1 has been completely written before it can begin. The constant write lock will starve any readers of the database.

A strategy to circumvent this is to ensure that write heavy operations go to different databases than read heavy operations. For example, there might be an application with the following scenario.

```
1  Analytics are written to the analytics database
2  User information and preferences are in the users database
```

This would ensure that operations against the users database would not be impacted by the heavy write operation against the analytics database.

 MongoDB 3.0 introduced collection level locking reducing the contention in a database by moving the lock level down to the individual collection. If we have heavy write to collection1 this does not cause looks for reads/writes to collection2.

7. WiredTiger Storage Engine

MongoDB 3.0 introduced an internal storage API, allowing for new storage engines to be added to MongoDB. MongoDB 3.0 included the new WiredTiger storage engine as an option. The WiredTiger storage engine brings a whole new set of possibilities when it comes to scaling MongoDB vertically. WiredTiger introduces document level locking and efficient CPU scaling. In this chapter, we provide an overview of the main aspects of the new storage engine.

7.1 Overview of WiredTiger

- Highly concurrent and vertically scalable
- Document level locking
- Allows for more tuning of storage engine than MMAP
- Compression
- On-line compaction
- Write-ahead transaction log for the journal
- Does not support in place updates

7.2 Essentials

The WiredTiger storage engine brings document level locking to MongoDB, meaning that writes no longer block a collection or database. While MMAP in 3.0 brought collection level locking, multiple writes to the same collection will still cause the writes to be applied serially and can starve reads from the collection as reads have to wait for the writes to finish. WiredTiger gets rid of the limitation allowing multiple writes to happen concurrently against the same collection. This means that writes and reads scale with the CPU, whereas in MMAP there was a low ceiling for CPU scaling as the locks reduced the throughput.

Another feature WiredTiger introduces, is on-disk compression supporting snappy and zlib. This allows the user to trade off CPU usage, for higher data compression.

Compression Methods

snappy	Balances the compression ratio with low CPU usage
zlib	Very good compression but comes at the cost of higher CPU usage than snappy

Compression is one of the major benefits of the WiredTiger engine, as it reduces the amount of data that needs to be written or read from the disk. This lowers the IO operations needed, and allows for better usage of the storage IO bandwidth available.

It also goes a far towards solving one of the main issues with MMAP which is the cost of storing all the document field names in each stored document as these are efficiently compressed. Indexes are also compressed using prefix compression, which allows for more of the index to be stored in RAM.

Although WiredTiger accepts two different on disk formats MongodDB officially only supports the Record Store engine in 3.0. The Record Store engine is a B+ tree and is optimized for read workloads.

Keep in mind is that WiredTiger does not support in place updates. In place updates will cause the whole document to be rewritten. Even though it does not allow for in place updates, it could still perform better than MMAP for many workloads. The additional vertical scalability might still offset the cost of writing the new documents.

For durability, WiredTiger uses a write ahead transaction log where a checkpoint is taken every 60 seconds or if 2GB are written. This is analogous to the MMAP disk flushing. In the worst case, if the mongodb process does you'll lose up to 60 seconds of data or 2GB.

7.3 Tuning

WiredTiger allows for tuning some of the storage engine parameters. The 3 most important to consider are the cache size, checkpoint interval and logging.

Cache Size

The cache size is the WiredTiger working set size. Initially it defaults to 50% or 1 GB which ever is the higher value.

Tuning the parameter can have a big impact on performance.

Checkpoint interval

The default checkpoint thresholds is 60 seconds, or 2GB data, whichever comes first. This setting can be changed to allow for more frequent, or less frequent checkpoints depending on the needs of the application, and what kind of durability guarantees you need.

Logging

WiredTiger uses a write-ahead log for the journaling that provides immediate write durability, with no need for `crash recovery`. One of the main things to keep in mind, is that the write-ahead log is not needed for `crash recovery`. `Crash recovery` is handled by the checkpoints mechanism. This stands in contrasts to MMAP where the journal is essential when performing `crash recovery`.

 If you are using a replicaset you might decide to turn off logging because replication is a good enough durability guarantee for you application.

7.4 When to use WiredTiger

This is one where it's best to benchmark your specific application, as it will vary depending on what kind of write and read patterns you application use, as well as the available hardware. For some workloads you might find that WiredTiger is a huge improvement, while for others there is no improvement, or even performance degradation. The schema simulator tool was specifically written to help you model and try your workload against MongoDB.

8. Indexes

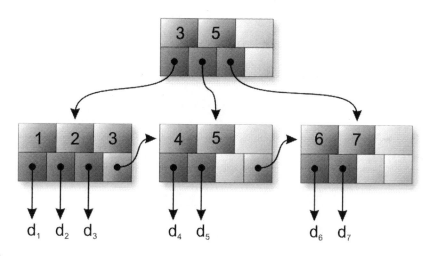

A Btree Example, http://commons.wikimedia.org/wiki/File:Btree.png

Indexes are key to achieving high performance in MongoDB, as they allow the database to search through less documents to satisfy a query. Without an index MongoDB has to scan through all of the documents in a collection to fulfill the query.

An index increases the amount of storage needed to represent a document and the time it takes to insert a document. Indexes trade off faster queries against storage space.

One of the principal things to remember about indexes, is that they are `inclusive`. `Inclusive` means they can only answer questions about documents that have been included in the index.

 Gotchas

$nin and $ne queries cannot be answered by indexes, and force collection scans. If you need to use these ensure you are filtering down using indexes as much as possible and leaving the $nin and $ne terms to the very last part of the query selector.

MongoDB has several types of indexes

- Single field indexes
- Compound indexes
- Multi key indexes
- Geo-spatial indexes
- Text indexes

It also supports a couple of variations of the above indexes

- Sparse indexes
- Unique indexes
- Time To Live indexes
- Covered Index Queries

8.1 Single field indexes

Take the following document

An example document

```
1  {
2    _id: ObjectId("523cba3c73a8049bcdbf6007"),
3    name: 'Peter Jackson',
4    age: 50,
5    nationality: "New Zealand",
6    address: {
7      street: "Some Street 22"
8    },
9    department: {
10     floor: 1,
11     building: 1
12   }
13 }
```

Let's look at some different ways we can apply a single field index

Example 1: A single field index

```
1  var values = db.getSisterDB("indexes").values;
2  values.ensureIndex({name: 1});
```

This indexes the name field in ascending order.

Example 2: A single embedded field index

```
1  var values = db.getSisterDB("indexes").values;
2  values.ensureIndex({"address.street": 1});
```

This indexes the street field, in the embedded document, under the address field.

Example 3: A embedded document field index

```
1  var values = db.getSisterDB("indexes").values;
2  values.ensureIndex({department: 1});
```

This indexes the department embedded document, allowing for strict equality matches on the it. It will only match on the query for a embedded document, that contains all the fields in the indexed embedded document.

Example 4: Embedded document match

```
1  var values = db.getSisterDB("indexes").values;
2  values.findOne({department: {floor: 1, building: 1}});
```

8.2 Compound indexes

A compound index is an index that contains references to multiple fields within a document.

Example 5: Create compound index

```
1   var values = db.getSisterDB("indexes").values;
2   values.ensureIndex({nationality: 1, age: -1, name: 1});
```

The compound indexes have some interesting properties. The index is usable if you have a query that includes nationality, age and name. But it's also able to answer other queries using the index.

1. Any query starting with nationality
2. Any query starting with nationality and age
3. Any query starting with nationality, age and name
4. Any query starting with nationality and name

For compound indexes order matters as we match from left to right. For example if you reverse a query to start with name and age, it will not match the order of fields in the compound index, and MongoDB will not be able to use the index to speed up the query.

Compound Index Field Order

Always make sure the order of fields in a compound index matches the order of fields in the queries you want to execute against the collection.

One thing to note about using a compound index is sorting. The ordering and direction of the fields in a compound index not only decide if it's possible to use the index in the query, but are also used for sorting.

Given the index {nationality: 1, age: -1, name: 1}, we can support the following sorting leveraging the index.

Example 6: Create compound index

```
1  var values = db.getSisterDB("indexes").values;
2  values.find().sort({nationality: 1, age: -1}).toArray();
3  values.find().sort({nationality: -1, age: 1}).toArray();
4  values.find().sort({nationality: -1, age: 1, name: -1}).toArray();
5  values.find().sort({nationality: 1, age: -1, name: 1}).toArray();
```

Sorting can only use the index if they match the order specified or the exact reverse order specified.

8.3 Multi key indexes

Multi key indexes lets MongoDB index arrays of values. Take the following example document.

Sample document

```
1  {
2    "title": "Superman",
3    "tags": ["comic", "action", "xray"],
4    "issues": [
5      {
6        "number": 1,
7        "published_on": "June 1938"
8      }
9    ]
10 }
```

Multi key indexes lets us search on the values in the tags array, as well as in the issues array. Let's create two indexes to cover both.

Example 7: Create Multikey fields

```
1  var comics = db.getSisterDB("store").comics;
2  comics.ensureIndex({tags: 1});
3  comics.ensureIndex({issues: 1});
```

The two indexes lets you do exact matches on values in the tags and issues arrays of values.

Example 8: Query using Multikey indexes

```
1  var comics = db.getSisterDB("store").comics;
2  comics.find({tags: "action"});
3  comics.find({issues: {number: 1, published_on: "June 1938"}}).toArray();
```

The first query will use the index on tags to return the document. The second will use the index on issues to return the document. The second query is dependent on the order of the fields in the documents indexed. If the number and published_on on fields changed order, the second query would fail.

If the document changes structure over time, it would be better to create a specific compound index on the fields needed in the embedded documents. A better index would be:

Example 9: Create Embedded Array Compound Index

```
1  var comics = db.getSisterDB("store").comics;
2  comics.ensureIndex({"issues.number":1, "issues.published_on":1});
```

To leverage the index, the second query can be written as follows.

Example 10: Query using the Compound Multikey index

```
1  var comics = db.getSisterDB("store").comics;
2  comics.find({
3    "issues.number":1,
4    "issues.published_on": "June 1938"}).toArray()
```

8.4 Geo-spatial indexes

MongoDB offers several Geo-spatial index types. These indexes make it possible to perform efficient Geo-spatial queries.

 GEO JSON

MongoDB supports GEO JSON (http://geojson.org) for performing GEO location queries.

Specialized 2d Sphere index

The 2d Geo-spatial Sphere index, allows applications to perform queries on an earth-like sphere, making for higher accuracy in matching locations.

Take the following example document.

A Simple document with location information

```
1  {
2    loc: {
3      type: "Point",
4      coordinates: [60, 79]
5    },
6    type: "house"
7  }
```

Create a 2dsphere index.

Example 11: Create 2dsphere compound index

```
1   var locations = db.getSisterDB("geo").locations;
2   locations.ensureIndex({loc: "2dsphere", house: 1});
```

Query the index using a GEO JSON type.

Example 12: Query using 2dsphere index

```
1    var locations = db.getSisterDB("geo").locations;
2    locations.find({loc: {
3        $geoWithin: {
4          $geometry: {
5            type: "Polygon",
6            coordinates: [[
7              [ 0 , 0 ] , [ 0 , 80 ] , [ 80 , 80 ] , [ 80 , 0 ] , [ 0 , 0 ]
8            ]]
9          }
10       }
11   }}).toArray();
```

Gotchas 2dsphere

The 2d sphere index is a pure GeoSpatial index and is limited to the ranges for latitude (-90 to 90) and longitude (-180 to 180). It also only accepts $geometry queries. In return it's faster and more accurate than the general 2d index.

General 2d index

The 2d index is a flat index that does not take into consideration any projection. One of the benefits of the 2d index is that it allows for fixed lower and upper bounds for the coordinate system as well as the search resolution. This makes for a more general 2d index.

Let's add a sample document.

A Simple document with location information

```
1   var houses = db.getSisterDB("2d").houses;
2   houses.insert({
3     price_rooms: [10000, 3],
4     type: "house"
5   });
```

Notice that the `price_rooms` is just an array. This is because the 2d index is not inherently tied to the GeoJSON format in the same way as the 2dsphere index.

Let's create a 2d index.

Example 13: Create 2d index

```
1   var houses = db.getSisterDB("2d").houses;
2   houses.ensureIndex({price_rooms: "2d"}, { min: 0, max: 200000, bits: 32 });
```

Now let's look for all houses that fall inside the range of 2000 to 20000 in price and have 0 to 5 rooms.

Example 14: Query for matching houses

```
1   db.houses.find( { price_rooms :
2     { $geoWithin : {
3        $box : [ [ 2000 , 0 ] , [ 20000 , 5 ] ]
4     }
5   }
6   }).toArray();
```

2d indexes

The `min` and `max` values let you project any 2d data with numeric values into a 2d index, where you can use geo queries like $near, $box etc to cut and slice the data. Once one realizes it's a generalized 2d index, it becomes quite useful for a range of queries not easily achieved with the standard query operators.

8.5 Text indexes

Text search is integrated into the MongoDB query language from version 2.6 (In 2.4 it was available as beta command). It relies on an underlying text index.

Let's insert some sample documents.

Insert some sample documents

```
1   var entries = db.getSisterDB("blogs").entries;
2   entries.insert( {
3     title : "my blog post",
4     text : "I'm writing a blog. yay",
5     site: "home",
6     language: "english" });
7   entries.insert( {
8     title : "my 2nd post",
9     text : "this is a new blog I'm typing. yay",
10    site: "work",
11    language: "english" });
12  entries.insert( {
13    title : "knives are Fun",
14    text : "this is a new blog I'm writing. yay",
15    site: "home",
16    language: "english" });
```

Let's create the text index.

Example 14: Create text index

```
1   var entries = db.getSisterDB("blogs").entries;
2   entries.ensureIndex({title: "text", text: "text"}, { weights: {
3       title: 10,
4       text: 5
5     },
6     name: "TextIndex",
7     default_language: "english",
8     language_override: "language" });
```

The example shows how weights can be used to control the weighing of fields in subsequent queries against the index. In this case any search that matches title will be ranked higher than a match in the text field.

We also passed a name option that allows us to give the index a custom name.

The default_language option specifies that any document missing a specific language field should default to english.

The option language_override tells the text index to look for individual documents language definition under the language field. If the language field for a specific document is set to for example Spanish, MongoDB will index it using the Spanish stop list and stemming.

Now let's query for all the blog entries that contain the blog word, and filter by the site field.

Example 15: Query using text index

```
1  var entries = db.getSisterDB("blogs").entries;
2  entries.find({$text: {$search: "blog"}, site: "home"})
```

The query matches all the documents, that contain the word blog in either the title or text field, and then filters them by the site field. If you wish to retrieve the search score for each matching document, modify the query slightly.

Example 16: Query using text index

```
1  var entries = db.getSisterDB("blogs").entries;
2  entries.find({$text: {$search: "blog"}, site: "home"},
3    {score: {$meta: "textScore"}}).sort({score: {$meta: "textScore"}});
```

The query includes the score given to the individual matched documents and sorts them in descending order by the score.

Text Indexes Can Get Big

Text indexes can grow to be bigger than the actual stored documents, and can take a while to build if the collection is big. They also add additional overhead to writes, compared to simpler indexes.

8.6 Sparse indexes

Sparse indexes are indexes, where no values are included for fields that do not exist. Look at the following two documents.

Sample documents

```
1  var sparse = db.getSisterDB("indexes").sparse;
2  sparse.insert({ hello: "world", number: 1 });
3  sparse.insert({ hello: "world" });
```

A non-sparse index for the field number, will contain an entry for both documents in the index. A sparse index will contain only the documents that contain the number field. Sparse indexes can be an efficient way of indexing fields that only occur in a certain percentage of documents in a collection, saving disk IO and memory.

To create a sparse index:

Example 17: Create Sparse Index

```
1  var sparse = db.getSisterDB("indexes").sparse;
2  sparse.ensureIndex({number: 1}, {sparse: true});
```

8.7 Unique indexes

An unique index is different from a normal index in that it only allows a single document to exist for a field value.

Example 18: Create Unique Index

```
1  var unique = db.getSisterDB("indexes").unique;
2  unique.ensureIndex({number: 1}, {unique: true});
```

Now let's try to insert some documents

Sample documents

```
1  var unique = db.getSisterDB("indexes").unique;
2  unique.insert({ hello: "world", number: 1 });
3  unique.insert({ hello: "world", number: 1 });
```

The second insert fails, due to the existing document with the field number set to 1.

8.8 Time To Live indexes

Time to live indexes (TTL) are a special type of index that will remove documents that fail to meet the index condition. One use for TTL indexes is to model a cache where documents expire after a set amount of time, allowing old documents to be gradually removed by MongoDB. This avoids the need of performing bulk deletes of documents using an external application or script.

Let's insert some documents.

Sample documents

```
1  var ttl = db.getSisterDB("indexes").ttl;
2  ttl.insert({ created_on: new Date() });
```

Let's define an a TTL index on created_on with an expire time of 1000 seconds in the future.

Example 19: Create TTL index

```
1  var ttl = db.getSisterDB("indexes").ttl;
2  ttl.ensureIndex({created_on: 1}, {expireAfterSeconds: 1000});
```

The TTL will delete any documents where the created_on field is older than 1000 seconds.

Notes about TTL

The `expireAfterSeconds` is not a hard limit. MongoDB will remove any expired documents some time after they have meet the condition.

It's important to note that Time to Live indexes only with *Date* based fields.

8.9 Covered Index Queries

Covered index queries are queries that can be answered using only the information stored in the index. Basically MongoDB answers the query using the fields stored in an index, never actually materializing the document into memory. Let's look at an example usage of covered queries.

Sample documents

```
1   var covered = db.getSisterDB("indexes").covered;
2   covered.insert({ text: "hello", site: "home"});
3   covered.insert({ text: "hello", site: "work" });
```

Let's define the covered index first.

Example 20: Create Covered index

```
1   var covered = db.getSisterDB("indexes").covered;
2   covered.ensureIndex({text: 1, site: 1});
```

Next perform a covered index query.

Example 21: Query using Covered Index

```
1   var covered = db.getSisterDB("indexes").covered;
2   covered.find({text: "hello"}, {_id: 0, text:1, site:1});
```

Let's retrieve the query plan.

Example 22: Query with Explain

```
1  var covered = db.getSisterDB("indexes").covered;
2  covered.find({text: "hello"}, {_id: 0, text:1, site:1}).explain();
```

This returns a result with all the details about the query plan executed for this query.

Query plan example, field removed for brevity

```
1  {
2    "cursor" : "BtreeCursor text_1_site_1",
3    "isMultiKey" : false,
4    "n" : 2,
5    "nscannedObjects" : 0,
6    "nscanned" : 2,
7    "nscannedObjectsAllPlans" : 0,
8    "nscannedAllPlans" : 2,
9    "scanAndOrder" : false,
10   "indexOnly" : true,
11   "nYields" : 0,
12   "nChunkSkips" : 0,
13   "millis" : 0,
14   ...
15   "server" : "christkv.local:27017"
16 }
```

Notice how the query plan result includes indexOnly set to true. This means that the query was completely covered by the index and MongoDB never touched the documents.

Covered Index Gotchas

Notice how {_id: 0, text:1, site:1} excludes _id. A covered index query cannot include the _id field.

9. Sharding

Sharding is one of the more complex features provided by MongoDB and getting comfortable with it can take some time. Sharding is a mechanism for scaling writes by distributing them across multiple shards. Each document contains an associated shard key field that decides on which shard the document lives.

9.1 Sharding Topology

In MongoDB sharding happens at the `collection` level. That is to say you can have a combination of `sharded` and `unsharded` collections. Let's look at a simple example topology.

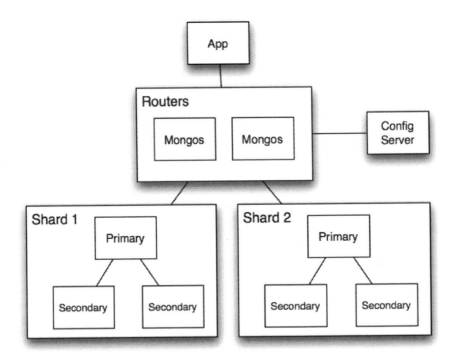

Simple Two Shard Topology

The application does not directly talk to the `shards` but instead talks through the `sharding` proxy *Mongos. Mongos* is responsible for the routing of writes and queries to the shards.

9.2 When to Shard

One of the typical errors people commit is to shard too early. The reason this can be a problem, is that sharding requires the developer to pick a shard key for distribution of the writes and it's easy to pick the wrong key early on due to not knowing how the data will be accessed over time.

This can lead reads to be inefficiently spread out across shards causing unnecessary IO and CPU usage in order to retrieve the data. Once the collection is sharded, it can be very time consuming to undo it, as all the data will have to be migrated from one sharded collection to another by reinserting all the documents into the new collection.

That said, let's look at some reason you might want to Shard.

1. Your Working Set no longer fits in the memory of your server. In this case, sharding can help make more of your Working Set stay in memory by pooling the RAM of all the shards. If you have a 20GB Working Set on a 16GB machine, sharding can split this across 2 machines for a total of 32GB of RAM available, potentially keeping all of the data in RAM and avoiding disk IO.
2. Scaling the write IO. You need to perform more write operations than what a single server can handle. By Sharding you can scale out the writes across multiple computers, increasing the total write throughput.

9.3 Choosing a Shard Key

It's important to pick a Shard key based on the actual read/write profile of your application to avoid inefficient queries and write patterns. There are a couple of tips that can help in the quest to identify the right shard key.

Easily Divisible Shard Key (Cardinality)

When discussing cardinality in the context of MongoDB, we refer to the ability to partition data into chunks distributed across all the shards. Let's look at some example shard keys.

Picking the state field as a shard key

In our documents the state field contains the US state for a specific address. This field is considered low cardinality, as all documents containing the same state will have to reside on the same shard. Since the key space for states is a limited set of values, MongoDB might end up distributing the data unevenly across a small set of fixed chunks. This might cause some unintentional side effects.

- It could lead to un-splittable chunks that could cause migration delays and unnecessary IO due to MongoDB attempting to split and migrate chunks.
- The un-splittable chunks might make it difficult to keep the shards balanced,causing load distribution to be uneven across the shards.
- If the number of values map to a maximum of un-splittable chunks, adding more shards might not help as there are fewer chunks available than shards. Due to the chunks being un-splittable, we cannot leverage the additional shards.

Picking the post code field as a shard key

If we pick the post code field as a shard key, the number of possible post codes is higher than when using the state state field. So the shard key is considered to have a higher cardinality than when using the state field. However the number of post codes does not completely mitigate the situation of un-splittable chunks. As one can imagine, one post code has a lot more associated addresses, which could make that specific chunk un-splittable.

Picking the phone number field as a shard key

The phone number field has high cardinality as there might be few users mapping to a specific phone number. This will make it easy for MongoDB to split chunks, as chunks won't be made up of documents that map to the same shard key, avoiding the possible problem of using the state field.

 Cardinality

Always consider the number of values your shard key can express. A sharding key that has only 50 possible values, is considered low cardinality, while one that might be able to express several million values might be considered a high cardinality key. High cardinality keys are preferable to low cardinality keys to avoid un-splittable chunks.

High Randomness Shard Key (Write Scaling)

A key with high randomness will evenly distribute the writes and reads across all the shards. This works well if documents are self contained entities such as Users. However queries for ranges of documents, such as all users with ages less than 35 years will require a scatter gather query where all shards are queried and a merge sort is done on Mongos.

Single Shard Targeted Key (Query Isolation)

Picking a shard key, that groups the documents together will make most of the queries go to a specific Shard. This can avoid scatter gather queries. One possible example might be a Geo application for the UK, where the first part of the key includes the postcode and the second is the address. Due to the first part of the shard key being the postcode, all documents for that particular sort key will end up on the same Shard, meaning all queries for a specific postcode will be routed to a single Shard.

The UK postcode works as it has a lot of possible values due to the resolution of postcodes in the UK. This means there will only be a limited amount of documents in each chunk for a specific postcode. However, if we were to do this for a US postcode we might find that each postcode includes a lot of addresses causing the chunks to be hard to split into new ranges. The effect is that MongoDB is less able to spread out the documents and in the end this impacts performance.

9.4 Routing Shard Keys

Depending on your Shard key the routing will work differently. This is important to keep in mind as it will impact performance.

Type Of Operation	Query Topology
Insert	Must have the Shard key
Update	Can have the Shard key
Query with Shard Key	Routed to nodes
Query without Shard Key	Scatter gather
Indexed/Sorted Query with Shard Key	Routed in order
Indexed/Sorted Query without Shard Key	Distributed sort merge

9.5 Inbox Example

Imagine a social Inbox. In this case we have two main goals

1. Send new messages to it's recipients efficiently
2. Read the Inbox efficiently

We want to ensure we meet two specific goals. The first one is to write to multiple recipients on separate shards thus leveraging the write scalability. For for a user to read their email box, one wants to read from a single shard avoid scatter/gather queries.

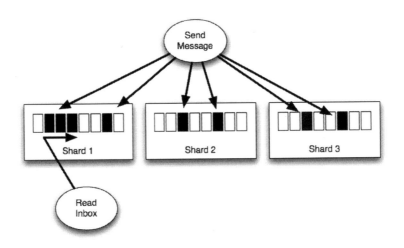

Fan out write, Single shard Read

How does one go about getting the correct shard key? Let's assume we have two collections inbox and users, in our social database.

Example 1: Shard the social collections

```
1  var db = db.getSisterDB('social');
2  db.shardCollection('social.inbox', {owner: 1, sequence: 1});
3  db.shardCollection('social.users', {user_name: 1});
```

Let's write and read to the collections with some test data to show how we can leverage the sharding.

Example 2: Write Email, Read Inbox

```
1   var db = db.getSisterDB('social');
2   var msg = {
3     from: 'Christian',
4     to: ['Peter', 'Paul'],
5     sent_on: new Date(),
6     message: 'Hello world'
7   }
8
9   for(var i = 0; i < msg.to.length; i++) {
10    var result = db.users.findAndModify({
11      query: { user_name: msg.to[i] },
12      update: { '$inc': {msg_count: 1} },
13      upsert: true,
14      new: true
15    })
16
17    var count = result.msg_count;
18    var sequence_number = Math.floor(count/50);
19    db.inbox.update({ owner: msg.to[i], sequence: sequence} ),
20      { $push: {messages: msg} },
21      { upsert:true });
22  }
23
24  db.inbox.find({owner: 'Peter'})
25    .sort({sequence: -1})
26    .limit(2);
```

The first part delivers the message to all its recipients. First, it updates the message count for the recipient and then pushes the message to the recipient's mailbox (which is an embedded document). The combination of the Shard key being {owner: 1, sequence: 1}, means that all new messages get written to the same chunk for a specific owner. The Math.floor(count/50) generation will split up the inbox into buckets of 50 messages in each.

This last aspect means that the read will be routed directly to a single chunk on a single Shard, avoiding scatter/gather and speeding up retrieval.

9.6 Multiple Identities Example

What if we need to lookup documents by multiple different identities like a user name, or an email address?

Take the following document:

Sample document

```
1  var db = db.getSisterDB('users');
2  db.users.insert({
3    _id: 'peter',
4    email: 'peter@example.com'
5  })
```

If we shard by _id, it means that only _id queries will be routed directly to the right shard. If we wish to query by email we have to perform a scatter/gather query.

There is a possible solution called document per identity. Let's look at a different way of representing the information.

Example 3: Set up Identities

```
1   var db = db.getSisterDB('users');
2
3   db.identities.ensureIndex({ identifier: 1 }, { unique: true });
4
5   db.identities.insert({
6     identifier: {user: 'peter'}, id: 'peter'});
7
8   db.identities.insert({
9     identifier: {email: 'peter@example.com', user: 'peter'},
10    id: 'peter'});
11
12  db.shardCollection('users.identities', {identifier: 1});
13  db.users.ensureIndex({ _id: 1}, { unique: true });
14  db.shardCollection('users.users'. { _id: 1});
```

We create a unique index for the `identities` table to ensure we cannot map two entries into the same identity space. Using the new compound shard key we can retrieve a user by its email by performing two queries. Let's see how we can look up the user document of the user with the email address of `peter@example.com`.

Example 4: Set up Identities

```
1   var db = db.getSisterDB('users');
2
3   var identity = db.identities.findOne({
4     identifier: {
5       email: 'peter@example.com'}});
6
7   var user = db.users.find({ _id: identity.id });
```

The first query locates the identity using the email, which is a routed query to a single shard. The second query uses the returned `identitiy.id` field to retrieve the user by the shard key.

9.7 Sharding Anti-Patterns

There are a couple of sharding anti-patterns that you should keep in mind to avoid some of the more common pitfalls.

Monotonically increasing shard key

A monotonically increasing shard key, is an increasing function such as a counter or an ObjectId. When writing documents to a sharded system using an incrementing counter as it's shard key, all documents will be written to the same shard and chunk until MongoDB splits the chunk and attempts to migrate it to a different shard. There are two possible simple solutions to avoid this issue.

Hashing the shard key

From MongodDB 2.4, we can tell MongoDB to automatically hash all of the shard key values. If we wanted to create documents where the shard key is _id with an ObjectId, we could shard the collection using the following options.

Example 5: Shard using hashed _id

```
1    sh.shardCollection( "users.users", { _id: "hashed" } )
```

Pre-split the chunks

The second alternative is to pre-split the shard key ranges and migrate the chunks manually, ensuring that writes will be distributed. Say you wanted to use a date timestamp as a shard key. Everyday you set up a new sharded system to collect data and then crunch the data into aggregated numbers before throwing away the original data.

We could pre-split the key range so each chunk represented a single minute of data.

Example 6: Shard using _id field

```
1   / first switch to the data DB
2   use data;
3   // now enable sharding for the data DB
4   sh.enableSharding("data");
5   // enable sharding on the relevant collection
6   sh.shardCollection("data.data", {"_id" : 1});
7   // Disable the balancer
8   sh.stopBalancer();
```

Let's split the data by minutes.

Example 7: Pre-split

```
1   / first switch to the admin db
2   use admin;
3   // 60 minutes in one hour, 24 hours in a day
4   var numberOfMinutesInDay = 60*24;
5   var date = new Date();
6   date.setHours(0);
7   date.setMinutes(0);
8   date.setSeconds(0);
9
10  // Pre-split the collection
11  for(var i = 0; i < numberOfMinutesInDay; i++) {
12    db.runCommand({ split: "data.data",
13      middle: {_id: date}
14    });
15
16    date.setMinutes(date.getMinutes() + 1);
17  }
```

Finally re-enable the balancer and allow MongoDB to start balancing the chunks to the shards.

Example 8: Enable balancer

```
1  // Enable the balancer
2  sh.startBalancer();
```

You can monitor the migrations by connecting to mongos, using the mongo shell and executing the sh.status() command helper to view the current status of the sharded system.

The goal of pre-splitting the ranges is to ensure the writes are distributed across all the shards even though we are using a monotonically increasing number.

10. Schema Design

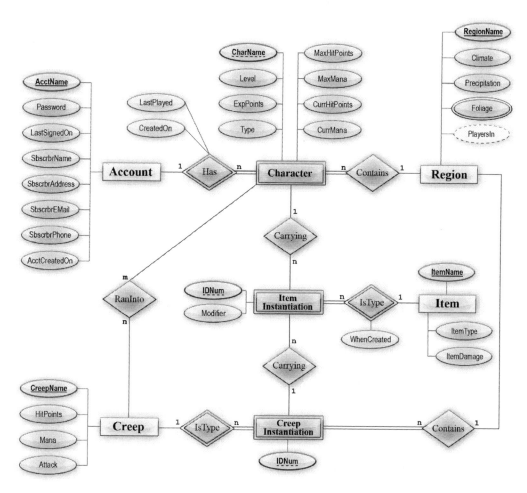

A Schema, http://upload.wikimedia.org/wikipedia/commons/7/72/ER_Diagram_MMORPG.png

There are several things to keep in mind when designing a schema for your application.

10.1 Read Ratio to Write Ratio

Determining if your application is read heavy or write heavy will lead to how you design your schema. If your application is read heavy, you might want to choose a schema that minimizes the amount of reads from MongoDB.

As an example consider an auction type website. As most operations are read operations caused by people browsing the catalog, it might makes sense to use a denormalized schema for the product including as much relevant information as needed to render the entire product page.

Similarly if your application is write heavy, you might want to ensure that you use a schema that maximizes MongoDB write throughput.

10.2 Avoid Application Joins

MongoDB does not support server side joins. All joins have to be performed in the application itself. The performance can suffer if you are pulling back and joining a lot of data due to all the round-trips required to bring back all the data and the time it takes to perform the in application join. If you find your schema is depending on a lot of joins, it might make sense to denormalize the schema in order to reduce the number of joins.

10.3 Pre-aggregate Data

Additionally, if you find you are aggregating data in a lot of application queries, you might want to consider pre-aggregating. One example might be a page view counter. Instead of summing up the number of views for a particular page on request, we can increment a view counter for that page each time the page is viewed and use this counter to show the number of page views.

10.4 Avoid Growing Documents (MMAP)

If, you find that your schema design creates documents that are constantly growing in size, it will have impact on your disk IO and database performance. Using document `buckets` and document `pre-allocation` will help address the issues for the MMAP storage engine.

10.5 Avoid Updating Whole Documents (MMAP)

MongoDB provides for atomic operators that let you modify fields in an existing document, and in most cases will cause an in-place update when using the MMAP storage engine. This ensures we spend as little time as possible re-allocating documents in memory and improves write performance.

10.6 Pre-allocated Documents (MMAP)

If your schema grows to a known size you can avoid document moves by pre-allocating the maximum size of the document causing all operations on the document to be in-place updates.

10.7 Field Names Take up Space (MMAP)

In some cases documents can contain more space allocated for the field names than the actual data stored. For this case you may want to consider compressing your field names if you are using MMAP or switch to using `WiredTiger` that supports compression using `snappy` or `zlib`.

10.8 Over Eager Indexing

You might get tempted to add all kinds of indexes to your schema. You have to keep in mind, that each index will impact performance, as they will need to be updated when documents change and the more indexes you have on a collection the more overhead there will be for each write operation. Each index also takes up space and memory so keep in mind that over eager indexing can cause your storage size to balloon.

10.9 Custom _id Field

You can save some space and additional indexes by overriding the meaning of the _id field. The only requirement is that _id is a unique field for the collection. For example you might have a structure that contains a timestamp, userid and machineid allowing you to use the _id index to query for those fields without having to create an additional index.

10.10 Covered Indexes

If your application can leverage covered indexes, it might help performance given that a query might be completely answerable using the data stored in the index without materializing the underlying documents.

11. Queue

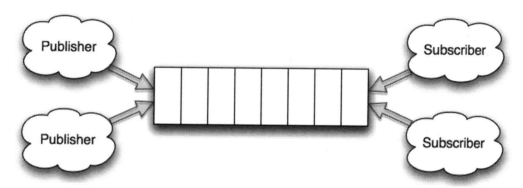

A Queue With Publishers and Subscribers

A queue in the setting of MongoDB, means a collection where inserted documents are kept in an order, either by the creation data of the document or by a priority assigned to the document. Multiple publishers can be inserting new documents into the queue at the same time, but each document can only be delivered to a single listener.

The queue schema introduced in this chapter is a work queue that is used to enqueue work for a set of listening processes. A job is represented by a document and can be dequeued either in FIFO (first in first out) order or by priority.

11.1 Schema Observations

- Efficient retrieval of queue jobs.
- Flexible.
- Easily adaptable to increased performance using an index.
- Relies on findAndModify, which means it's imperative that the query aspect of the operation is as efficient as possible in order to minimize write locks (less of an issue with WiredTiger).
- Potentially read and write intensive.

11.2 Schema

Schema Attributes	
Optimized For	Write/Read Performance

The schema expressed here only contains the minimal set of fields needed to represent work items. One of the things omitted, is the ability to identify what process is working on a specific item. There is also no additional meta data provided about the work item itself.

Example 1: The fields in a job document and their types

```
1   {
2       'startTime': date
3     , 'endTime': date
4     , 'createdOn': date
5     , 'priority': number
6     , 'payload': object
7   }
```

For this schema we will use the following fields.

Field	Description
startTime	The time the job was started
endTime	The time the job ended
createdOn	The time the document was created
priority	A numeric priority where a higher value is higher priority
payload	An embedded document that is the work payload

One could easily extend the schema by adding a process_id field that could contain the information about what listener picked up the document.

11.3 Operations

Let's look at the different operations we can perform on the queue schema.

Inserting a Job

Inserting a job into the work queue is fairly simple and straight forward using the shell as an example.

Example 2: Insert a sample job document

```
1  var col = db.getSisterDB("work").queue;
2  col.insert({
3      'startTime': null
4    , 'endTime': null
5    , 'createdOn': new Date()
6    , 'priority': 1
7    , 'payload': {
8        'type': 'convertImage'
9      , 'source': '/images/image.png'
10     , 'output': '/images/image.jpg'
11   }
12 });
```

In this example, we insert a new job that converts images from one type to another.

Return the next FIFO Job

If we wish to fetch the next item using FIFO, we can do this in the following way.

Example 3: Fetch a job FIFO style

```
1   var col = db.getSisterDB("work").queue;
2   var job = col.findAndModify({
3       query: {startTime: null}
4     , sort: {createdOn: 1}
5     , update: {$set: {startTime: new Date()}}
6     , new: true
7   });
```

This query will retrieve the document with the oldest createdOn data, and set the startTime field to the current Date, before returning the updated document.

findAndModify

One thing to remember is that findAndModify takes a write lock for the duration of the operation. What this means in practice, is that it will not allow concurrent writes to happen while the operation is in process. The impact of this lock depends on the version of MongoDB.

MongoDB 2.6 and earlier have a db level lock that will block the database for write operations. MongoDB 3.0 improves on this for the MMAP engine by making it a collection level lock. If you use the WiredTiger storage engine it only requires a document level lock.

It's important to ensure there is an index on createdOn to reduce the total time the findAndModify operation takes to execute.

Return the Highest Priority Job

To fetch a job sorted by the highest priority and created date, we perform a slightly different query to the FIFO one.

Example 4: Fetch the next highest priority job

```
1  var col = db.getSisterDB("work").queue;
2  var job = col.findAndModify({
3      query: {startTime: null}
4    , sort: {priority: -1, createdOn: 1}
5    , update: {$set: {startTime: new Date()}}
6    , new: true
7  });
```

This query differs from the FIFO one in a particular way. First, we sort by priority and then perform a secondary sorting on createdOn.

Finishing a Job

When we have finished processing a job we simply update the job endTime, signaling that the job was done.

Example 5: Set a job as finished

```
1  var col = db.getSisterDB("work").queue;
2  col.update({_id: job._id}, {$set: {endTime: new Date()}});
```

We look up the job by using the `job._id` field and set the `endTime` field to the current data and time.

11.4 Indexes

There are a couple of indexes that we can create to help performance with this schema. Let's look at what kind of queries we are performing for the queue schema.

Return the next FIFO Job

The query is {startTime: null} and we sort by {createdOn:1}. To effectively use an index, we can create a composite index featuring the two fields. This allows both the query and sort to each use an index.

Example 6: Create the FIFO index

```
var col = db.getSisterDB("work").queue;
col.ensureIndex({startTime: 1, createdOn: 1});
```

When executing the query part of the findAndModify with the explain command:

Example 7: Query with query plan

```
var col = db.getSisterDB("work").queue;
col.find({startTime: null}).sort({createdOn: 1}).explain()
```

The result field cursor contains the text BtreeCursor showing that the query has executed using an index. In our case the cursor field looked like this.

```
"cursor" : "BtreeCursor startTime_1_createdOn_1"
```

This is the expected outcome, as we wish to avoid performing a collection level scan. Here, the worst case scenario is an index scan for all entries where startTime is null.

Return the highest Priority Job

The query is slightly different from the FIFO one, as we involve three different fields. The query is {startTime: null} is the same as the FIFO query, but the sort includes both the priority and createdOn fields {priority: -1, createdOn: 1}. This particular query benefits from a compound index containing all three fields. Let's create the index using *ensureIndex*.

Example 8: Create the FIFO index

```
1  var col = db.getSisterDB("work").queue;
2  col.ensureIndex({startTime: 1, priority: -1, createdOn: 1});
```

Execute the query part of the findAndModify with explain

Example 9: Query with query plan

```
1  var col = db.getSisterDB("work").queue;
2  col.find({startTime: null}).sort({priority: -1, createdOn: 1}).explain()
```

Just as with the FIFO query, we see that the cursor field returned contains the word BtreeCursor. In our case it comes back looking like this.

```
"cursor" : "BtreeCursor startTime_1_priority_-1_createdOn_1"
```

This is the expected outcome as we wish to avoid performing a collection level scan. Here, the worst case scenario is an index scan for all entries where startTime is null.

TTL Indexes

MongoDB 2.4 or higher has a new type of index called TTL, that lets the server remove documents gradually over time. Let's look at an example document.

Example 10: An example job document

```
{
    'startTime': ISODate("2014-01-01T10:02:22Z")
  , 'endTime': ISODate("2014-01-01T10:06:22Z")
  , 'createdOn': ISODate("2014-01-01T10:01:22Z")
  , 'priority': 1
  , 'payload': {
      'type': 'convertImage'
    , 'source': '/images/image.png'
    , 'output': '/images/image.jpg'
  }
}
```

We want to only keep the last 24 hours worth of jobs once they are finished. Before MongoDB 2.4 the only way to accomplish this would be to perform a batch remove using a script or application.

With the introduction of the TTL index, we can let MongoDB perform the deletion of documents for us avoiding additional code and the possible interruptions to write performance bulk deletes might cause. Creating the TTL index is very straightforward.

Example 11: Add a TTL index to collection

```
1  var db = db.getSisterDB("data");
2  var numberOfSeconds = 60 * 60 * 24; // 60 sec * 60 min * 24 hours
3  db.expire.ensureIndex({ "endTime": 1}, {expireAfterSeconds: numberOfSeconds })
```

This creates a TTL index on the endTime field that will remove any documents where the endTime field is older than 24 hours.

Time To Live Indexes (TTL)

The TTL index is not a hard real-time limit. It only guarantees that documents will be expired some time after they hit the expire threshold, but this period will vary depending on the load on MongoDB and other currently running operations.

11.5 Scaling

Secondary Reads

All the operations against the queue are write operations so secondary reads are not useful for this schema.

Sharding

Both the FIFO and priority based queues use findAndModify querying on startTime equal to null. If we used startTime as the shard key the findAndModify will fail as it attempts to set the startTime field which is immutable as it's the shard key. There is no real way around this so sharding does not make sense for this particular schema.

If you wish to scale the schema, you can do this by creating multiple collections and assigning the collections to separate shards thus spreading the writes across multiple MongoDb servers.

11.6 Performance

Performance is limited to the amount of time it takes for the findAndModify to finish. With the MMAP storage engine the lock level is db level in 2.6 and collection level in 3.0. For WiredTiger the document level locking means that performance is less impacted by findAndModify.

A simple exploration of the performance on a single machine with MongoDb 3.0 shows the difference between MMAP and WiredTiger for a narrow simulation using the schema simulation framework mongodb-schema-simulator.

Scenario

---

https://github.com/christkv/mongodb-schema-simulator/blob/master/examples/simulations/queue_fifo_simulation.js

MongoDb runs locally on a MacBook Pro Retina 2015 with ssd and 16 gb ram. The simulation runs with the following parameters against a single mongodb instance under osx 10.10 Yosemite.

Parameters

processes	4
poolSize per process	50
type	linear
Resolution in milliseconds	1000
Iterations run	25
Total number of users publishing per iteration	1000
Total number of users reading per iteration	300
Execution strategy	slicetime

Warning

 ## This is not a performance benchmark

The graphs here are shown to give an understanding of the difference between the two storage engines available and **IS NOT** indicative of the performance obtained on a real production system. Furthermore more it's important to understand that MongoDB is not optimized for osx.

The mongodb-schema-simulator tool was made expressively so you can simulate these schemas yourself on your own hardware.

MMAP

The MMAP engine is run using the default settings on MongoDB 3.0.1.

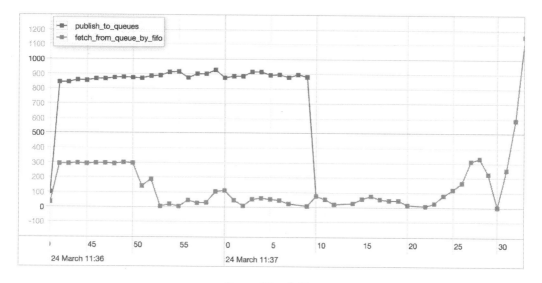

Queue Simulation

publish_to_queues scenario results

Statistics

Runtime	52.289 seconds
Mean	31.288 milliseconds
Standard Deviation	21.479 milliseconds
75 percentile	48.616 milliseconds
95 percentile	55.736 milliseconds
99 percentile	59.138 milliseconds
Minimum	0.401 milliseconds
Maximum	77.987 milliseconds

fetch_from_queue_by_fifo scenario results

Statistics	
Runtime	52.289 seconds
Mean	15195.361 milliseconds
Standard Deviation	13526.237 milliseconds
75 percentile	28049.003 milliseconds
95 percentile	33552.295 milliseconds
99 percentile	35403.374 milliseconds
Minimum	1.233 milliseconds
Maximum	37248.023 milliseconds

What we can observe here is the cost of the collection level write lock in MMAP as all the writes get priority over the reads swamping the server and limiting read throughput. As the writes tail off, the queued reads start getting through but due to the large backlog the average time of the reads increases dramatically in comparison to the writes.

WiredTiger

The WiredTiger engine is run using the default settings on MongoDB 3.0.1.

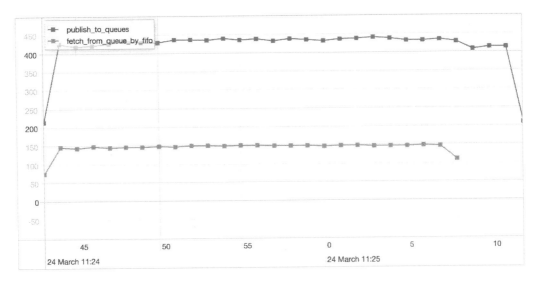

Queue Simulation

publish_to_queues scenario results

Statistics

Runtime	31.113 seconds
Mean	32.455 milliseconds
Standard Deviation	44.732 milliseconds
75 percentile	51.322 milliseconds
95 percentile	127.275 milliseconds
99 percentile	188.452 milliseconds
Minimum	0.412 milliseconds
Maximum	312.698 milliseconds

fetch_from_queue_by_fifo scenario results

Statistics

Runtime	31.113 seconds
Mean	48.493 milliseconds
Standard Deviation	718.43 milliseconds
75 percentile	5.873 milliseconds
95 percentile	10.658 milliseconds
99 percentile	29.38 milliseconds
Minimum	1.329 milliseconds
Maximum	19499.33 milliseconds

We can see the benefit of document level locking here as the writes are spread out more evenly across the whole runtime when `WiredTiger` yields to reads. However, the improvement is not huge and it comes with a much bigger cpu overhead. `WiredTiger` does not support inplace updates and has to copy the data for each `findAndModify` that is performed.

11.7 Notes

Picking the right storage engine for the schema is imperative. Although `WiredTiger` is somewhat faster in this scenario it's important to consider its higher cpu usage and the fact that it does not support in place updates which could impact performance depending on the size of the document.

12. Topics

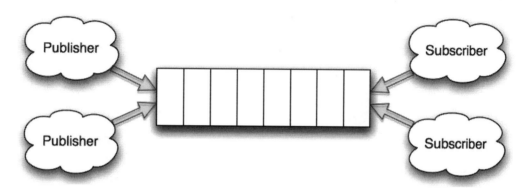

A Queue With Publishers and Subscribers

A topic-based system is one where messages are published to a named channel (topics) to one or more subscribers. The difference from a queue is that all subscribers receive the same message.

MongoDB has a special type of collection called a `capped` collection, and a special type of cursor called a `tailable` cursor, that lets you simply and elegantly model a topic-based publish and subscribe system.

A `capped` collection is basically a ring buffer, meaning they are a fixed size in bytes. As we insert documents into the capped collection, they are added one after the other in the buffer, until we reach the end of the buffer. Once it gets to the end of the buffer, it wraps around and starts overwriting the documents at the start of the buffer.

The main benefit of a `capped` collection is that it allows for a `tailing` cursor, meaning applications can get notified as new documents are inserted into the collection.

The first limitation of a `capped` collection is that inserted documents cannot grow. If you need to change the shape of a document, you will need to insert a pre-padded document to ensure your document does not grow outside the allocated space.

The second limitation of `capped` collections is that they are in-memory structures only. So if the MongoDB server is shutdown, you will loose the content of the `capped` collection. The capped collections, will however replicate across to secondaries in a replicaset. If you need fail over support, it's recommended to deploy a replicaset.

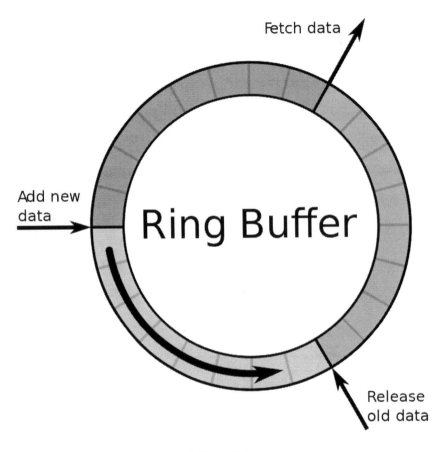

A Ring Buffer

In this chapter we will use a stock ticker for our topic schema example.

12.1 Schema Observations

- Leverages capped collections
- Works with replication
- Performs well
- To many listeners impact CPU usage on MongoDB currently (MongoDB 3.0 or earlier).
- Collection is not persistent. If the mongodb process dies, the capped collection is gone. Use a replicaset to avoid this problem.
- Potentially read and write heavy.

12.2 Schema

Schema Attributes	
Optimized For	Write Performance
Pre-Allocation	Only if the documents need to grow

We will use a very simplified stock ticker schema to showcase how topics can be created and used with MongoDB.

Example 1: A simple ticker document

```
{
  "time": ISODate("2014-01-01T10:01:22Z")
  "ticker": "PIP",
  "price": "4.45"
}
```

12.3 Operations

Create the capped collection

To create the capped collection, we need to use the createCollection command, passing the capped collection options.

Example 2: Create a capped collection

```
1  var db = db.getSisterDB("finance");
2  db.createCollection("ticker", {capped:true, size:100000, max: 100000})
```

The available options are:

Option	Type	Description
capped	boolean	Signal that we want to create a capped collection
autoIndexId	boolean	Create index for the _id field. Set to false when replicating the collection
size	number	The size of the capped collection in bytes in the collection before wrapping around
max	number	The maximum number of documents in the collection before wrapping around
usePowerOf2Sizes	boolean	Default allocation strategy from 2.6 and on

Creating Random Ticker Documents

Let's create some activity in our capped collection, by writing a publisher script. First boot up a new mongo shell and run a publisher that creates a new ticker document with a random price once a second.

Example 3: Create random ticker document every second

```
1   var db = db.getSisterDB("finance");
2   while(true) {
3     db.ticker.insert({
4       time: new Date(),
5       ticker: "PIP",
6       price: 100 * Math.random(1000)
7     })
8
9     sleep(1000);
10  }
```

Ticker Consumer

To consume the messages being published to the topic, let's write a consumer script. Boot up another mongo shell, and run a script that will consume messages from the topic.

Example 4: Start up a consumer

```
1  var db = db.getSisterDB("finance");
2  var cursor = db.ticker.find({time: {$gte: new Date()}}).addOption(DBQuery.Option.tail\
3  able).addOption(DBQuery.Option.awaitData)
4
5  while(cursor.hasNext) {
6    print(JSON.stringify(cursor.next(), null, 2))
7  }
```

The script will only receive tickers that are newer than the date and time the script was started.

12.4 Indexes

The indexes for this schema will vary by how you query the data in your consumers. In this simple stock ticker publisher/consumer, we can see that we query the collection by the time field. To avoid collection scans, we create an index on the time field.

Example 5: Create the time index

```
1  var col = db.getSisterDB("finance").ticker;
2  col.ensureIndex({time: 1});
```

12.5 Scaling

Secondary Reads

Secondary reads can help scale the number of subscribers. This allows an application to increase the number of listeners by distributing the read load across multiple secondaries.

Sharding

Capped collections do not support sharding.

12.6 Performance

Capped collections are in-memory collections and are limited to the speed of memory. Unfortunately, there is a performance limit caused by the way tailing cursors are currently implemented. As you add more and more tailing cursors, the MongoDB cpu usage increases markedly. This means that it's important to keep the number of listeners low to get better throughput.

If you are just pulling data off the topic, and not performing any modifications to the documents using secondary reads with a replicaset might help scale the number of listeners you can deploy without creating undue cpu usage on the servers.

A simple exploration of the performance on a single machine with MongoDb 3.0 shows the difference between MMAP and WiredTiger for a narrow simulation using the schema simulation framework mongodb-schema-simulator.

Scenario
https://github.com/christkv/mongodb-schema-simulator/blob/master/examples/simulations/topic_simulation.js

MongoDb runs locally on a MacBook Pro Retina 2015 with ssd and 16 gb ram. The simulation runs with the following parameters against a single mongod instance under osx 10.10 Yosemite.

Parameters	
processes	4
poolSize per process	50
type	linear
Resolution in milliseconds	1000
Iterations run	25
Total number of users publishing per iteration	1000
Total number of users listening to topic	40
Execution strategy	slicetime, custom

Parameters

MMAP

The MMAP engine is run using the default settings on MongoDB 3.0.1.

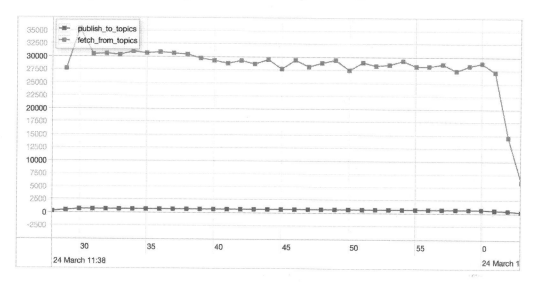

Topics Simulation

publish_to_topics scenario results

Statistics

Runtime	44.39 seconds
Mean	2.616 milliseconds
Standard Deviation	7.824 milliseconds
75 percentile	2.318 milliseconds
95 percentile	5.523 milliseconds
99 percentile	21.792 milliseconds
Minimum	0.703 milliseconds
Maximum	420.747 milliseconds

fetch_from_topics scenario results

Statistics

Runtime	44.39 seconds
Mean	0.001 milliseconds
Standard Deviation	0.003 milliseconds
75 percentile	0.002 milliseconds
95 percentile	0.004 milliseconds
99 percentile	0.02 milliseconds
Minimum	~0.00 milliseconds
Maximum	0.323 milliseconds

There doesn't seem to much to note here. The writes per second is pretty much exactly 1000, mirroring the number of concurrent users we have defined in the simulation. As the capped collection is in-memory, the writing speed is limited only to MongoDB's lock handling and memory performance.

One thing to keep in mind, is that before MongoDB 3.0 the MMAP engine only supported db level locking which meant it was better to place a high throughput capped collection in its own separate database. In MongoDB 3.0 the MMAP engine lowers the lock level to collection level which means it can coexist with other collections in the same database without impacting other collections with lock contention.

WiredTiger

The WiredTiger engine is run using the default settings on MongoDB 3.0.1.

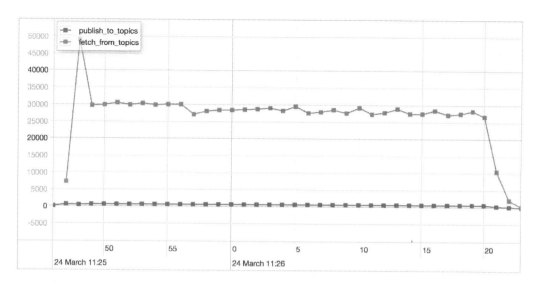

Topics Simulation

publish_to_topics scenario results

Statistics

Runtime	45.39 seconds
Mean	2.848 milliseconds
Standard Deviation	11.15 milliseconds
75 percentile	2.432 milliseconds
95 percentile	5.699 milliseconds
99 percentile	22.597 milliseconds
Minimum	0.740 milliseconds
Maximum	522.21 milliseconds

fetch_from_topics scenario results

Statistics

Runtime	45.39 seconds
Mean	0.001 milliseconds
Standard Deviation	0.004 milliseconds
75 percentile	0.002 milliseconds
95 percentile	0.004 milliseconds
99 percentile	0.020 milliseconds
Minimum	~0.00 milliseconds
Maximum	0.363 milliseconds

WiredTiger does not really make a big difference here compared to MMAP as the back end storage system is memory and not disk. Remember that WiredTiger supports document level locking. So there is no need to take into consideration placing the capped collection in its own separate db to avoid lock contention, as for MMAP pre MongoDB 3.0.

12.7 Notes

Capped collection can be extremely useful to create topic like systems, where you have multiple publishers and subscribers. However due to the current limitations on how tailed cursors work in MongoDB currently, it's important to balance the number of active listeners with the cpu usage.

13. Metadata

Metadata, courtesy of http://www.flickr.com/photos/sjcockell/6126442977

Metadata is data that describes and provides information about other data. A classic example is the information about a digital photo, such as the ISO settings, resolution, pixel depth, exposure, camera settings, camera type and so on.

Let's look at some sample metadata for an image.

Field	Value
File name	img_1771.jpg
File size	32764 Bytes
MIME type	image/jpeg
Image size	480 x 360
Camera make	Canon
Camera model	Canon PowerShot S40
Image timestamp	2003-12-14 12-01-44
Image number	117-1771
Exposure time	1/500 s
Aperture	F4.9
Exposure bias	0 EV
Flash	No, auto

Each image might contain a different mix of fields depending on what features the camera supports. A cell phone might add GPS coordinates as metadata, while another might add more detailed flash information.

Obviously, it's unfeasible to create an index for each possible metadata field. The schema we present in this chapter is optimized to allow for quick and efficient retrieval of documents by metadata fields.

13.1 Schema Observations

- Efficiently query in diverse sets of metadata tags, using a single index.
- All metadata keys are represented in the index, meaning it can get fairly large.
- Optimized for a read heavy workload.

13.2 Schema

In our schema we are going to leverage the fact that one can index arrays of objects easily in MongoDB. By using this ability, we can create a metadata field in a document, that can be efficiently queried.

Example 1: A document containing the metadata schema

```
1   {
2     "metadata": [
3       {"key": "File Name", "value": "img_1771.jpg"},
4       {"key": "File size", "value": 32764},
5       {"key": "MIME type", "value": "image/jpeg"},
6       {"key": "Image size", "value": {"width": 480, "height": 360}},
7       {"key": "Camera make", "value": "Canon"},
8       {"key": "Camera model", "value": "Canon PowerShot S40"},
9       {"key": "Image timestamp", "value": ISODate("2014-01-01T10:01:00Z")},
10      {"key": "Image number", "value": "117-1771"},
11      {"key": "Exposure time", "value": "1/500 s"},
12      {"key": "Aperture", "value": "F4.9"},
13      {"key": "Exposure bias", "value": "0 EV"},
14      {"key": "Flash", "value": "No, auto"}
15    ]
16  }
```

13.3 Operations

To correctly query this schema, we need to learn about two query selection operators that allow us to match embedded documents in an array.

$all

The $all query operator is defined as selecting all the documents where the value of a field is an array that contains all the specified elements.

Example 2: A simple $all query example

```
1   var col = db.getSisterDB("supershot").images;
2   col.findOne({tags: {$all: [ "appliance", "school", "book" ]}});
```

$elemMatch

The $elemMatch query operator matches more than one component within an array element.

Example 3: A simple $elemMatch query example

```
1  var col = db.getSisterDB("supershot").images;
2  col.findOne({metadata: {$elemMatch: {key: "File Name", value: "img_1771.jpg"}}});
```

Let's see how we can use the two operators to locate documents in our metadata schema.

The $elemMatch operator looks like the obvious first choice. However, the problem is that our metadata array is defined as objects that all have key and value fields. If you attempt to enter multiple matches using key and value in the $elemMatch only the last pair will be used.

If we wish to locate a photo that has MIME type equal to image/jpeg, and also Flash equal to No, auto we need to combine the two query operators $all and $elemMatch.

Let's take a look at how to query our desired documents.

Querying Documents by Multiple metadata fields

Example 4: Locate images using multiple metadata fields

```
1  var col = db.getSisterDB("supershot").images;
2  col.find({ metadata: { $all: [
3              { "$elemMatch" : { key : "MIME type", value: "image/jpeg" } },
4              { "$elemMatch" : { key: "Flash", value: "No, auto" } }
5          ]}
6      }).toArray();
```

The first $elemMatch operator will locate all the documents with the MIME type equal to image/jpeg and then filter on the Flash key.

13.4 Indexes

To provide efficient retrieval of documents using the metadata schema, we need to create an index that allows us to optimize the query using the $elemMatch and $all operators.

For this we will need a compound index on the key and value fields inside the metadata array.

Example 5: Create index for metadata field

```
1  var col = db.getSisterDB("supershot").images;
2  db.images.ensureIndex({"metadata.key": 1, "metadata.value": 1});
```

13.5 Scaling

Secondary Reads

If the site is read heavy (say a photo album site), it might make sense to offload reads to secondary servers allowing the read load to be spread out.

Using secondary reads comes down to the level of acceptable latency for your application is willing to live with as there might be some delay between a write happening on a primary and the document being visible on the secondary.

Sharding

There is no efficient way to shard documents by a generic metadata key as the general nature of the schema precludes the usage of any of the fields in the metadata structure as a shard key.

The metadata would typically be part of the narrowing of a query and the shard key would be related to the purpose of the document containing the metadata structure.

Let's take the image example and amend it with a user Id. We'll would use the userId field as the shard key, route the query to a single shard and then narrow the query using the metadata fields.

```
 1   {
 2     , "userId": "olepeteraaa1"
 3     , "metadata": [
 4       {"key": "File Name", "value": "img_1771.jpg"},
 5       {"key": "File size", "value": 32764},
 6       {"key": "MIME type", "value": "image/jpeg"},
 7       {"key": "Image size", "value": {"width": 480, "height": 360}},
 8       {"key": "Camera make", "value": "Canon"},
 9       {"key": "Camera model", "value": "Canon PowerShot S40"},
10       {"key": "Image timestamp", "value": ISODate("2014-01-01T10:01:00Z")},
11       {"key": "Image number", "value": "117-1771"},
12       {"key": "Exposure time", "value": "1/500 s"},
13       {"key": "Aperture", "value": "F4.9"},
14       {"key": "Exposure bias", "value": "0 EV"},
15       {"key": "Flash", "value": "No, auto"}
16     ]
17   }
```

> **ℹ** Using the userId as the shard key will ensure user specific images will be located on the same shard.

13.6 Performance

A simple exploration of the performance on a single machine with MongoDb 3.0 shows the difference between MMAP and WiredTiger for a narrow simulation using the schema simulation framework mongodb-schema-simulator.

Scenario

https://github.com/christkv/mongodb-schema-simulator/blob/master/examples/scripts/single_or_replset/metadata_access_scenario.js

MongoDb runs on a MacBook Pro Retina 2013 with 512 GB ssd and 16 gb ram. The simulation runs with the following parameters against a single mongodb instance under osx 10.10 Yosemite.

Parameters

processes	4
poolSize per process	50
type	linear
Resolution in milliseconds	1000
Iterations run	25
Number of users querying using metadata per iteration	1000
Execution strategy	slicetime

MMAP

The `MMAP` engine is run using the default settings on `MongoDB 3.0.1`.

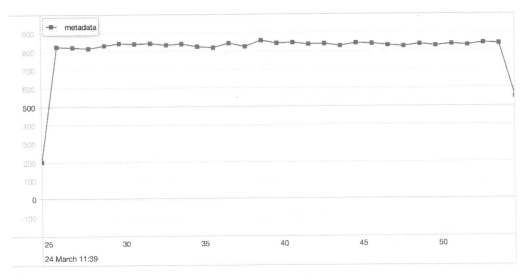

Metadata Read Simulation

metadata scenario results

Statistics
Runtime	40.874 seconds
Mean	0.954 milliseconds
Standard Deviation	0.291 milliseconds
75 percentile	1.187 milliseconds
95 percentile	1.367 milliseconds
99 percentile	1.619 milliseconds
Minimum	0.441 milliseconds
Maximum	4.885 milliseconds

As we can see the `1000` users a second impacts the minimum and maximum as well as the average query time a fair bit.

WiredTiger

The `WiredTiger` engine is run using the default settings on `MongoDB 3.0.1`.

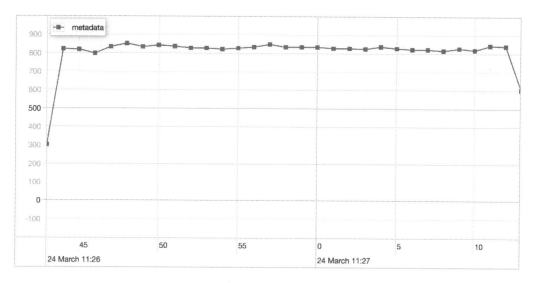

Metadata Read Simulation

metadata scenario results

Statistics

Runtime	40.01 seconds
Mean	0.992 milliseconds
Standard Deviation	0.318 milliseconds
75 percentile	1.232 milliseconds
95 percentile	1.431 milliseconds
99 percentile	1.706 milliseconds
Minimum	0.484 milliseconds
Maximum	9.827 milliseconds

As expected there is not much difference between the `MMAP` and `WiredTiger` storage engines since this is mainly a read only workload.

13.7 Notes

 Runtime versus Iterations

The number of iterations here is 25 meaning that every 1000 milliseconds we start up another 1000 users attempting to read metadata. We can see that the total runtime is around ~40 seconds instead of 25 seconds, which means we have surpased the maximum continous read capacity of the MongoDB instance on the used hardware. If we adjusted down the simulation load until the Runtime of the scenario was around ~25 seconds, we could estimate the maxmimum load our topology can handle.

14. Materialized Path Category Hierarchy

The nested categories schema design pattern targets the hierarchical tree structures traditionally found in a product catalog on an e-commerce website.

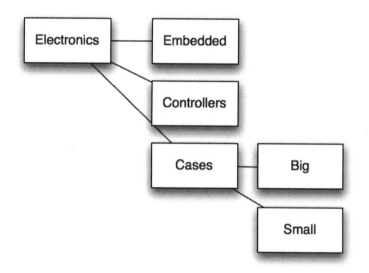

A Category Hierarchy Example

We'll will be presenting a pattern called the materialized path pattern. This pattern refers to categories by a file system like path concept `/monitors/lg/led`.

14.1 Schema Observations

- Allows for efficient retrieval of a category's direct children or subtree.

- Very flexible.
- Makes it easy to allow products to belong to multiple categories.
- Easily adaptable to increased performance using an index.
- Relies on regular expressions, making it more complicated (a wrong regular expression can easily cause a full collection scan)

14.2 Schema

Lets look at an example category document.

```
1  {
2      "_id": ObjectId("54fd7392742abeef6186a68e")
3    , "name": "embedded"
4    , "parent": "/electronics"
5    , "category": "/electronics/embedded"
6  }
```

Schema Attributes

name	Name of the category
parent	The parent category path. If the parent is the root it will be /
category	The current category path

Lets insert a stripped down product document.

```
1  {
2      "_id": ObjectId("54fd7392742abeef6186a68e")
3    , "name": "Arduino"
4    , "cost": 125
5    , "currency": "USD"
6    , "categories": ["/electronics/embedded"]
7  }
```

Schema Attributes

name	Name of the product
cost	The cost of the product
currency	The product currency
categories	An embedded array of category paths for this product. A product can belong to one or more categories

14.3 Operations

Find the direct ancestors of a specified category

We want to retrieve all the direct children categories of the /electronics category.

Example 1: Fetch direct children of /electronics category

```
1  var col = db.getSisterDB("catalog").categories;
2  var categories = col.find({parent: /^\/electronics$/});
```

Notice the regular expression /^\/electronics$/ that we're using. This translates as all documents, where the field **parent** starts with **/electronics** and ends with **/electronics**.

Find the subtree of a specific category

We want to retrieve the entire subtree of categories for the /electronics category.

Example 2: Fetch subtree of /electronics category

```
1  var col = db.getSisterDB("catalog").categories;
2  var categories = col.find({parent: /^\/electronics/});
```

Notice the regular expression /^\/electronics/ that we're using. This regular expression matches all documents where the field parent starts with /^\/electronics/. The effect is such that the query will return all the categories in the subtree below /electronics.

Find all products by category

It's fairly straightforward to query for products by a specific category, thanks to the embedded categories field.

Example 3: Fetch all products of /electronics/arduino category

```
1  var col = db.getSisterDB("catalog").products;
2  var products = col.find({categories: "/electronics/arduino"});
```

Find all the categories in the parent path for a specific category

To get all the categories in the parent path for a specific category, we need to do some preprocessing of the path for the specific category.

Example 4: Fetch root path of /electronics/embedded/arduino

```
1  var elements = '/electronics/embedded/arduino'.split('/');
2  var paths = [];
3
4  for(var i = 0; i < elements.length - 1; i++) {
5    elements.pop();
6    paths.push(elements.join('/'));
7  }
8
9  paths.push('/');
10 paths.reverse();
11
12 var col = db.getSisterDB("catalog").categories;
13 var products = col.find({ name: { $in: paths } });
```

In the example above, we created all the combinations of paths possible from the originating path /electronics/embedded/arduino by creating an array containing all the paths from the route the parent category of our provided path. In this case that becomes the array ['/', '/electronics', '/electronics/embedded'].

Find all the products for a category's direct children

If we wish to find all the products for a specific category's direct children, we have to first retrieve the category and then perform an $in query on the products collection.

Example 4: Fetch products of direct category children

```
1   var c = db.getSisterDB("catalog").categories;
2   var p = db.getSisterDB("catalog").products;
3   var categories = c.find({parent: /^\/electronics$/}).map(function(x) {
4       return x.category;
5   });
6   var products = p.find({ categories: { $in: categories } });
```

Find all the products in a category subtree

In order to locate all the products for a specific category's subtree, we need to first retrieve the category and then perform an $in query on the products collection.

Example 5: Fetch products of category subtree

```
1   var c = db.getSisterDB("catalog").categories;
2   var p = db.getSisterDB("catalog").products;
3   var categories = c.find({parent: /^\/electronics/}).map(function(x) {
4       return x.category;
5   });
6   var products = p.find({ categories: { $in: categories } });
```

14.4 Indexes

We retrieve categories by the parent and category fields. Let's ensure we can index on the category field as well as the parent field for the categories collection.

Example 6: Create the category field index

```
1  var col = db.getSisterDB("catalog").categories;
2  col.ensureIndex({category:1});
```

We also need to create an index for the parent field.

Example 7: Create the parent field index

```
1  var col = db.getSisterDB("catalog").categories;
2  col.ensureIndex({parent:1});
```

For the products collection we retrieve products by using the categories field. So, let's ensure we have an index for the categories field.

Example 8: Create the categories field index

```
1  var col = db.getSisterDB("catalog").products;
2  col.ensureIndex({categories:1});
```

14.5 Covered Index Queries

Covered index queries are queries that can be answered using only the information stored in the index. Basically MongoDB answers the query using the fields stored in an index but never actually materializes the document into memory. We could create a covered index for categories to allow for quick retrieval of a specific category path.

Example 9: Adding a covered index

```
1  var col = db.getSisterDB("catalog").categories;
2  col.ensureIndex({parent:1, name: 1})
```

The Index {parent:1, name:1} is a compound index and will contain both the parent and name fields, and can cover queries containing both those fields.

Let's rewrite the query of all the categories just below the top level /electronics and look at the explain plan.

Example 10: Query using covered index

```
1  var col = db.getSisterDB("catalog").categories;
2  col.find({parent: /^\/electronics$/}, {_id:0, parent:1, name:1}).explain();
```

This should return a document result that contains a field indexOnly that is set to true indicating that the query can be answered by only using the index. You will have to give up the _id field for this query. In many cases covered index queries can provide a significant performance boost over normal queries as it avoids accessing the documents during the read operation.

Knowing this we can rewrite the query for the direct sub categories of the path /electronics.

Example 11: Sub categories using covered index

```
1  var col = db.getSisterDB("catalog").categories;
2  var categories = col.find({parent: /^\/electronics/}, {_id:0, parent:1, name:1});
```

14.6 Scaling

Secondary Reads

In the case of a product catalog, secondaries might help the application scale its reads, given that most of the workload is read only. This allows the application to leverage multiple secondaries to increase read throughput. The trade off is that it might take some time for product document changes to replicate from the primary to the secondaries causing some stale reads. This might not be a problem but it's important to be aware of the trade-off.

Sharding

Sharding the product category may not be effective and in most circumstances sharding will not add much in the way of performance as the workload is mostly read only. It could be better to approach scaling using secondary reads.

14.7 Performance

A simple exploration of the performance on a single machine with MongoDb 3.0 shows the difference between `MMAP` and `WiredTiger` for a narrow simulation using the schema simulation framework `mongodb-schema-simulator`.

Scenario
https://github.com/christkv/mongodb-schema-simulator/blob/master/examples/scripts/single_or_replset/materialized_path_category_-hierarchy/retrieve_direct_child_categories_scenario.js https://github.com/christkv/mongodb-schema-simulator/blob/master/examples/scripts/single_or_replset/materialized_path_category_-hierarchy/retrieve_entire_sub_tree_by_category_scenario.js

MongoDb runs locally on a MacBook Pro Retina 2015 with ssd and 16 gb ram. The simulation runs with the following parameters against a single `mongodb` instance under `osx 10.10 Yosemite`.

Retrieve direct category children categories

Parameters	
processes	4
poolSize per process	50
type	linear
Resolution in milliseconds	1000
Iterations run	25
Number of users reading	1000
Execution strategy	slicetime

Retrieve category subtree

Parameters

processes	4
poolSize per process	50
type	linear
Resolution in milliseconds	1000
Iterations run	25
Number of users reading	1000
Execution strategy	slicetime

MMAP

The MMAP engine is run using the default settings on MongoDB 3.0.1.

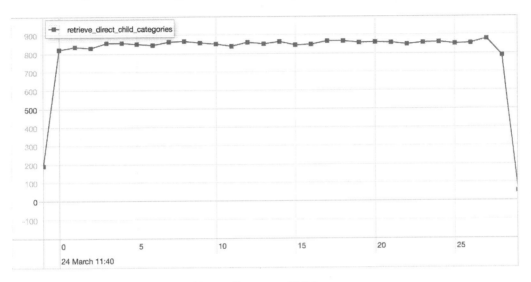

Direct Category Children

direct children results

Statistics

Runtime	31.773 seconds
Mean	0.954 milliseconds
Standard Deviation	0.357 milliseconds
75 percentile	1.162 milliseconds
95 percentile	1.630 milliseconds
99 percentile	1.998 milliseconds
Minimum	0.394 milliseconds
Maximum	7.196 milliseconds

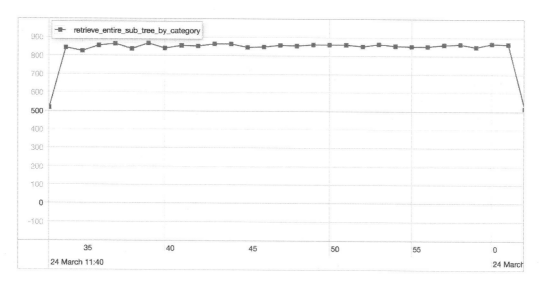

Category Subtree

category subtree results

Statistics

Runtime	31.617 seconds
Mean	0.963 milliseconds
Standard Deviation	0.413 milliseconds
75 percentile	1.159 milliseconds
95 percentile	1.669 milliseconds
99 percentile	2.104 milliseconds
Minimum	0.379 milliseconds
Maximum	8.818 milliseconds

WiredTiger

The `WiredTiger` engine is run using the default settings on `MongoDB 3.0.1`.

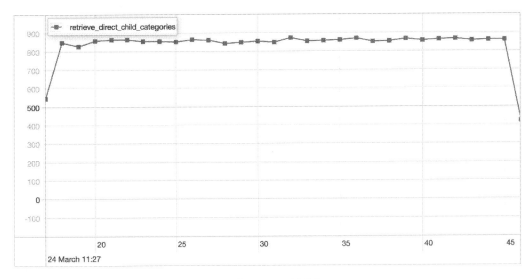

Direct Category Children

direct children results

Statistics

Runtime	31.187 seconds
Mean	0.998 milliseconds
Standard Deviation	0.417 milliseconds
75 percentile	1.187 milliseconds
95 percentile	1.874 milliseconds
99 percentile	2.247 milliseconds
Minimum	0.399 milliseconds
Maximum	7.093 milliseconds

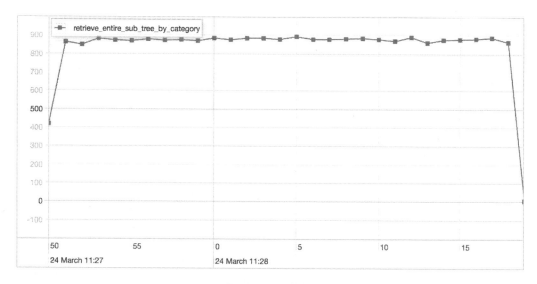

Category Subtree

category subtree results

Statistics

Runtime	30.584 seconds
Mean	0.992 milliseconds
Standard Deviation	0.495 milliseconds
75 percentile	1.183 milliseconds
95 percentile	1.886 milliseconds
99 percentile	2.386 milliseconds
Minimum	0.394 milliseconds
Maximum	19.589 milliseconds

As this is a read only workload the two storage engines are close in performance for the amount of load we applied to the MongoDB server instance.

14.8 Notes

One of the things to remember is that regular expression queries can only leverage indexes when they are *case insensitive* and convert to a simple start to end string match that can leverage an index. A more complex regular expression will cause a full index scan.

The following query will correctly use the index.

```
1   col.find({parent: /^\/electronics/}, {_id:0, parent:1, name:1}).explain();
```

The next query will cause an index scan due to it being a case insensitive regular expression.

```
1   col.find({parent: /^\/electronics/i}, {_id:0, parent:1, name:1}).explain();
```

If you can live with not retrieving the whole document for your category tree queries the covered indexes will allow you to avoid materializing the actual category documents into memory as the queries can be answered with the fields stored in the index itself.

15. Shopping Cart with Product Reservation

Metadata, courtesy of http://www.wpclipart.com/working/work_supplies/shopping_cart_racing.png.html

The traditional E-commerce shopping cart, allows the user to reserve products for a limited period of time, before releasing them back into inventory. This chapter will show you a possible way to model a shopping cart that reserves products using MongoDB.

15.1 Schema Observations

- Ensures that the system cannot sell more quantity of a product than is available in the inventory.
- Double bookkeeping means all transactions can be rolled back correctly.
- Requires background process that expires carts correctly and returns any reserved products to the inventory.
- Worst case scenario is that all the product inventory sits in the carts reserved until the carts expire and the reserved products are returned to the inventory.

15.2 Schema

The schema we will be using is a stripped down version of what a real e-commerce system would use, but serves to illustrate how to design a shopping cart with product reservation. We will be using four different collections. These are the carts, inventories, orders and products collections.

Let's look at an example cart that contains one product.

```
1   {
2       "_id": ObjectId("54fd7392742abeef6186a68e")
3     , "state": "active"
4     , "modifiedOn": ISODate("2015-03-11T12:03:42.615Z")
5     , "products": [{
6           "_id": ObjectId("54fd7392742abeef6186a68e")
7         , "quantity": 1
8         , "name": "JC Sneaker"
9         , "price": 100
10      }]
11  }
```

Below is an inventory document example that contains one reservation.

```
1   {
2       "_id": ObjectId("54fd7392742abeef6186a68e")
3     , "quantity": 999
4     , "reservations": [{
5           "_id": ObjectId("54fd7392742abeef6186a68e")
6         , "quantity": 1
7         , "createdOn": ISODate("2015-03-11T12:03:42.615Z")
8      }]
9   }
```

The cart and inventory schemas are used to perform double bookkeeping, which avoids the possibility of selling more inventory than what is actually available.

In the example inventory document shown, the total available stock is always the sum of the quantity field at the top level of the document and all the quantity fields in the embedded array reservations. In this case the total available product is

```
1  totalAvailableProduct = 99 + 1;
2  totalReservedProduct = 1;
```

Only after the cart has been successfully checked out do we remove the cart reservation from the reservations array, thus reducing the available total stock.

If the cart is canceled or times out, we can easily return the stock for the product by reversing the reservations made for the cart using the entries in the reservations array.

The last two schemas are the products and order schemas where products contains the product information and orders contains the resulting document from a successful shopping cart checkout.

Below is an example product document.

```
1  {
2      "_id": ObjectId("54fd7392742abeef6186a68e")
3      , "name": "JC Sneaker"
4      , "properties": {}
5  }
```

Example order schema with a single product.

```
1  {
2      "_id": ObjectId("54fd7392742abeef6186a68e")
3      , "total": 100
4      , "shipping": {}
5      , "payment": {}
6      , "products": [{
7          "_id": ObjectId("54fd7392742abeef6186a68e")
8          , "quantity": 1
9          , "name": "JC Sneaker"
10         , "price": 100
11      }]
12  }
```

15.3 Operations

Adding a product to the Shopping Cart

When the user attempts to reserve a specific quantity of a product, we need to perform 2 steps.

1. First add the item to the `products` array in the `cart` document for the user, creating the cart in the process, if one does not already exist.
2. Update the `inventory` document with the reservation, if there is enough quantity of the product available to cover the reservation.

When there is not enough inventory of the product available, we need to rollback the addition of the item to the cart.

Let's start by adding a product to the shopping cart. We are making some assumptions here in order to simplify the code. Those assumptions are that we have a `userId` of 1 and a `productId` of `111445GB3`;

Example 1: Add product to shopping cart

```
1   var quantity = 1;
2   var userId = 1;
3   var productId = "111445GB3";
4
5   var col = db.getSisterDB("shop").carts;
6   col.update(
7     { _id: userId, state: 'active' }
8     , {
9       $set: { modifiedOn: new Date() }
10      , $push: { products: {
11        _id: productId
12      , quantity: quantity
13      , name: "Simsong Mobile"
14      , price: 1000
15      }}
16   }, true);
```

The updated statement above performs an upsert. This means the document is created for the provided userId and state if one does not already exists.

The next step is to attempt to reserve the quantity of the product in the inventory collection.

Example 2: Reserve product inventory

```
1   var userId = 1;
2   var quantity = 1;
3
4   var col = db.getSisterDB("shop").inventories;
5   col.update({
6       _id: productId, quantity: { $gte: quantity }
7   }, {
8       $inc: { quantity: -quantity }
9     , $push: {
10      reservations: {
11        quantity: quantity, _id: userId, createdOn: new Date()
12      }
13    }
14  });
```

This will add the cart reservation to the reservations array for the product document only if there is enough quantity to satisfy the reservation request.

If there is not enough product quantity available in the inventory, we need to rollback the addition of the product to the cart.

Example 3: Rollback product addition

```
1   var userId = 1;
2   var quantity = 1;
3   var productId = "111445GB3";
4
5   var col = db.getSisterDB("shop").carts;
6   col.update({
7     _id: userId
8   }, {
9       $set: { modifiedOn: new Date() }
10    , $pull: { products: { _id: productId }}
11  })
```

We do this by finding the embedded document in the products array that has the _id field equal to the productId, and then removing it from the products array by using the $pull operator.

Updating the Reservation Quantity for a Product

If the user changes his mind about the amount of product he wishes to purchase, we need to update the amount of that product in the shopping cart as well as to ensure that there is sufficient inventory to cover the newly requested quantity.

First let's update the quantity in the shopping cart. We start by fetching the existing quantity. Then, we need to calculate the delta (the change between the old and new quantity). Finally we update the cart with the changes.

Example 4: Update product quantity in cart

```
1   var userId = 1;
2   var newQuantity = 2;
3   var productId = "111445GB3";
4
5   var col = db.getSisterDB("shop").carts;
6   var cart = db.findOne({
7       _id: userId
8     , "products._id": productId
9     , status: "active"});
10  var oldQuantity = 0;
11
12  for(var i = 0; i < cart.products.length; i++) {
13    if(cart.products[i]._id == productId) {
14      oldQuantity = cart.products[i].quantity;
15    }
16  }
17
18  var delta = newQuantity - oldQuantity;
19
20  col.update({
21      _id: userId
22    , "products._id": productId
23    , status: "active"
24  }, {
25    $set: {
```

```
26        modifiedOn: new Date()
27      , "products.$.quantity": newQuantity
28    }
29  });
```

Having updated the quantity in the cart, we now need to ensure there is enough product inventory available to cover the requested change in quantity. The additionally requested quantity is the difference between (newQuantity and oldQuantity).

Example 5: Reserve additional product inventory

```
1   var userId = 1;
2   var newQuantity = 2;
3   var productId = "111445GB3";
4
5   var col = db.getSisterDB("shop").products;
6   col.update({
7       _id: productId
8     , "reservations._id": userId
9     , quantity: {
10        $gte: delta
11    }
12  }, {
13    , $inc: { quantity: -delta }
14      $set: {
15        "reservations.$.quantity": newQuantity, modifiedOn: new Date()
16      }
17  })
```

This correctly reserves more product inventory, or returns any non-needed product inventory.

1. If, the delta is a *negative* number the $gte will always hold and the product quantity gets increased by the delta in effect returning product inventory.
2. If delta is a *positive* number the $gte will only hold if inventory is equal to delta. If the $gte condition is meet, the inventory is decreased by delta quantity, in effect reserving more product inventory.

If there is not enough inventory to fulfill the new reservation, we need to rollback the change we made to the cart. We do that by re-applying the old quantity.

Example 6: Rolling back quantity change request

```
1   var userId = 1;
2   var oldQuantity = 1;
3   var productId = "111445GB3";
4
5   var col = db.getSisterDB("shop").carts;
6   col.update({
7       _id: userId
8     , "products._id": productId
9     , status: "active"
10  }, {
11    $set: {
12        modifiedOn: new Date()
13      , "products.$.quantity": oldQuantity
14    }
15  });
```

Expiring Carts

It's common for customers to have put items in a cart and then abandon the cart. This means there is a need for a process to expire carts that have been abandoned. For each expired cart we need to.

1. Return the reserved items to the product inventory.
2. Mark the cart as expired.

Below is a script that will look for any cart that has been sitting inactive for more than 30 minutes. Any carts that are older than 30 minutes have their contents returned to their respective product inventories and are then marked expired.

Example 7: Expiring shopping carts

```
1   var cutOffDate = new Date();
2   cutOffDate.setMinutes(cutOffDate.getMinutes() - 30);
3
4   var cartsCol = db.getSisterDB("shop").carts;
5   var productCol = db.getSisterDB("shop").products;
6
7   var carts = cartsCol.find({
8       modifiedOn: { $lte: cutOffDate }, state: 'active'
9     });
10
11  while(carts.hasNext()) {
12    var cart = carts.next();
13
14    for(var i = 0; i < cart.products.length; i++) {
15      var product = cart.products[i];
16
17      productCol.update({
18          _id: product._id
19        , "reservations._id": cart._id
20        , "reservations.quantity": product.quantity
21      }, {
22          $inc: { quantity: product.quantity }
23        , $pull: { reservations: { _id: cart._id }}
24      });
25    }
26
27    cartsCol.update({
28      _id: cart._id
29    }, {
30      $set: { status: 'expired' }
31    });
32  }
```

For each cart, we iterate over all the products in the cart. For each of the products, we return the quantity to the product inventory and at the same time remove that cart from the reserved array of the product document.

After returning the inventory we set the status of the cart to expired. Notice that we don't clean up the cart document itself. We are keeping the expired cart as historic data.

Checkout

The customer clicked the checkout button on the website and entered their payment details. It's time to issue a purchase order, and clean up the cart and product reservations.

Example 8: Checking out shopping cart

```
1   var userId = 1;
2
3   var cartsCol = db.getSisterDB("shop").carts;
4   var productCol = db.getSisterDB("shop").products;
5   var orderCol = db.getSisterDB("shop").orders;
6
7   var cart = cartsCol.findOne({ _id: userId, state: 'active' });
8
9   orderCol.insert({
10      created_on: new Date()
11    , shipping: {
12        name: "Joe Dow"
13      , address: "Some street 1, NY 11223"
14    }
15    , payment: { method: "visa", transaction_id: "2312213312XXXTD" }
16    , products: cart.products
17  });
18
19  cartsCol.update({
20    { _id: userId }
21  }, {
22    $set: { status: 'complete' }
23  });
24
25  productCol.update({
26    "reservations._id": userId
27  }, {
28    $pull: { reservations: {_id: userId }}
29  }, false, true);
```

We perform the following actions during checkout

1. Add a finished order document to the orders collection representing the payed for order.

2. Set the cart to done status
3. Remove the cart from the reservations arrays of all products where it's present using a multi update.

15.4 Indexes

For the carts collection we reference carts by the state field to find expired carts. We can add an index for this field to make the query more efficient.

Example 9: Create the state field index

```
1  var col = db.getSisterDB("catalog").carts;
2  col.ensureIndex({state:1});
```

For the inventories collection we look up embedded documents in the reservations array by the _id field. We need to create a multi key index for this field.

Example 10: Create the reservations._id field index

```
1  var col = db.getSisterDB("catalog").inventories;
2  col.ensureIndex({"reservations._id":1});
```

For the products and orders collections we do not need any other indexes than the default _id for our limited examples.

15.5 Scaling

Secondary Reads

All the operations against the cart are write operations so secondary reads are not useful for this schema as they might show out of date carts.

Sharding

Sharding the carts is fairly straight forward as each cart is self-contained so the easiest shard key for this is a hashed _id key. This allows for the writes to be distributed as randomly as possible across all the shards.

Example 11: Hashed _id shard key

```
var admin = db.getSisterDB("admin");
db.runCommand({enableSharding:'shop'});
db.runCommand({
    shardCollection: 'shop.carts'
  , key: {_id:'hashed'}
});
```

15.6 Performance

A simple exploration of the performance on a single machine with MongoDb 3.0 shows the difference between MMAP and WiredTiger for a narrow simulation using the schema simulation framework mongodb-schema-simulator.

Scenario

https://github.com/christkv/mongodb-schema-simulator/blob/master/examples/scripts/single_or_replset/cart_reservation/cart_5_-item_reservation_successful_scenario.js

MongoDb runs locally on a MacBook Pro Retina 2015 with ssd and 16 gb ram. The simulation runs with the following parameters against a single mongodb instance under osx 10.10 Yosemite.

successfully checkout cart parameters

Parameters	
processes	4
poolSize per process	50
type	linear
Resolution in milliseconds	1000
Iterations run	25
Number of products in cart	5
Size of each product in bytes	1024
Number of users	1000

Parameters

Execution strategy	slicetime

MMAP

The MMAP engine is run using the default settings on MongoDB 3.0.1.

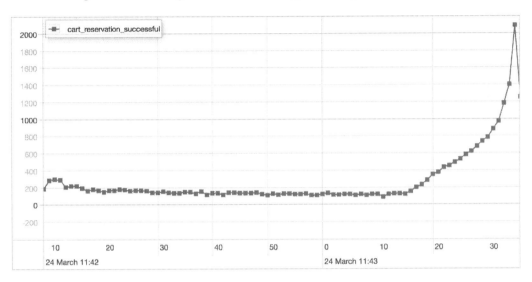

Successfully Checkout Cart

successfully checkout cart

Statistics

Runtime	88.241 seconds
Mean	46416.268 milliseconds
Standard Deviation	21937.134 milliseconds
75 percentile	62873.337 milliseconds
95 percentile	67818.018 milliseconds
99 percentile	70497.126 milliseconds
Minimum	20.034 milliseconds
Maximum	74220.014 milliseconds

WiredTiger

The WiredTiger engine is run using the default settings on MongoDB 3.0.1.

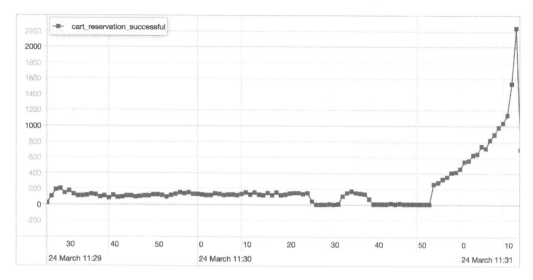

Successfully Checkout Cart

successfully checkout cart

Statistics

Runtime	108.916 seconds
Mean	63597.036 milliseconds
Standard Deviation	27672.244 milliseconds
75 percentile	83614.989 milliseconds
95 percentile	87405.772 milliseconds
99 percentile	89546.218 milliseconds
Minimum	41.414 milliseconds
Maximum	93681.381 milliseconds

This is an `update` heavy schema and this impacts WiredTiger more than `MMAP` due to a lack of in place updates in `WiredTiger`. Also note that the total runtime is higher than the 25 seconds' of load we apply, pointing to the fact that the system is overloaded for this hardware configuration.

15.7 Notes

The reservation of items using an embedded array in an `inventory` document could lead to the size of the document growing a fair bit if there are a lot of shoppers reserving the same product at the same time. In these cases, we recommend the optimistic shopping cart pattern reviewed in the next chapter.

16. Shopping Cart with No Product Reservation

Metadata, courtesy of http://www.wpclipart.com/working/work_supplies/shopping_cart_racing.png.html

This shopping cart schema more closely resembles the amazon shopping cart. When you add products to the cart, they are not reserved. The actual check for product inventory is only performed when the user checks out the cart.

16.1 Schema Observations

- No locking up of product inventory until the checkout process allows for simple scaling of shopping cart schema.
- Amazon style shopping cart.
- No reservations means the user will not know if reservation of product inventory was successful until checkout time.

16.2 Schema

The schema we will be using is a stripped down version of what a real e-commerce system would use. It serves the purpose of illustrating the concepts needed to design a shopping cart with no product reservation. There are four collections we are interested in for our schema. These are the carts, inventories, orders and products collections.

Let's look at an example cart that contains one product.

```
1   {
2      "_id": ObjectId("54fd7392742abeef6186a68e")
3    , "state": "active"
4    , "modifiedOn": ISODate("2015-03-11T12:03:42.615Z")
5    , "products": [{
6         "_id": ObjectId("54fd7392742abeef6186a68e")
7       , "quantity": 1
8       , "name": "JC Sneaker"
9       , "price": 100
10      }]
11  }
```

Example inventory document that contains one reservation

```
1   {
2      "_id": ObjectId("54fd7392742abeef6186a68e")
3    , "quantity": 999
4    , "reservations": [{
5         "_id": ObjectId("54fd7392742abeef6186a68e")
6       , "quantity": 1
7       , "createdOn": ISODate("2015-03-11T12:03:42.615Z")
8      }]
9   }
```

The main difference from the previous cart schema is that we do not reserve any product inventory until the very end when the user checks out the cart.

The last two collections are the products and order collection. The products collection contains the product information and the orders collection contains the final order document resulting from a successful shopping cart checkout.

Below is an example product document.

```
1  {
2      "_id": ObjectId("54fd7392742abeef6186a68e")
3      , "name": "JC Sneaker"
4      , "properties": {}
5  }
```

Example order document with a single product.

```
1   {
2       "_id": ObjectId("54fd7392742abeef6186a68e")
3       , "total": 100
4       , "shipping": {}
5       , "payment": {}
6       , "products": [{
7           "_id": ObjectId("54fd7392742abeef6186a68e")
8           , "quantity": 1
9           , "name": "JC Sneaker"
10          , "price": 100
11      }]
12  }
```

16.3 Operations

Adding a product to the Shopping Cart

When the user attempts to reserve a quantity of a particular product in our application we just need to perform a single step in comparison to the reservation based cart schema.

Simply add the item to the products array in the cart document for the user creating the cart if one does not already exist.

Let's take a look at how we go about adding the product to the cart. We are going to make some assumptions to simplify the example code. Those assumptions are that we have a userId of 1 and a productId of 111445GB3;

Example 1: Add product to shopping cart

```
1   var quantity = 1;
2   var userId = 1;
3   var productId = "111445GB3";
4
5   var col = db.getSisterDB("shop").carts;
6   col.update(
7       { _id: userId, state: 'active' }
8     , {
9         $set: { modifiedOn: new Date() }
10      , $push: { products: {
11          _id: productId
12        , quantity: quantity
13        , name: "Simsong Mobile"
14        , price: 1000
15      }}
16    }, true);
```

The updated statement above performs an upsert, meaning the document is created if one does not already exist for the provided userId and state.

Updating the Reservation Quantity for a Product

If the user decides to change the quantity for a specific product in the cart, we only need to change the product quantity in the cart.

Example 2: Update product quantity in cart

```
1   var quantity = 2;
2   var userId = 1;
3   var productId = "111445GB3";
4
5   var col = db.getSisterDB("shop").carts;
6   col.update(
7       { _id: userId, "products._id": productId, state: 'active' }
8     , {
9         $set: {
10            modifiedOn: new Date()
11          , "products.$.quantity": quantity
```

```
12        }
13      }
14    }, true);
```

There is no need to update any inventory for this case or perform any rollbacks.

Checkout

The core of the logic here is in the checkout method. At the time of checkout, we need to attempt to reserve all requested inventory for all products in the cart.

Example 3: Attempt to reserve the inventory

```
1    var userId = 1;
2
3    var inventories = db.getSisterDB("shop").inventories;
4    var carts = db.getSisterDB("shop").carts;
5    var orders = db.getSisterDB("shop").orders;
6
7    var cart = carts.find({_id: userId});
8    var success = [];
9    var failed = [];
10
11   for(var i = 0; i < cart.products.length; i++) {
12     var product = cart.products[i];
13
14     var result = inventories.update({
15         _id: product._id, quantity: {$gte: product.quantity }
16       }, {
17           $inc: {quantity: -product.quantity}
18         , $push: {
19           reservations: {
20             quantity: product.quantity, _id: cart._id, createdOn: new Date()
21           }
22         }
23       })
24
25     if(result.nModified == 0) failed.push(product);
26     else success.push(product);
27   }
```

For each product in the shopping cart, we attempt to reserve inventory for it. If the reservation attempt fails, we add the failed product to the array called `failed` and if it's successful, we add the product to the `success` array.

In the end, if there are any products in the `failed` array, we need to rollback all the successful reservations into the `inventories` collection.

Example 4: Rollback inventory reservation attempt

```
if(failed.length > 0) {
  for(var i = 0; i < success.length; i++) {
    inventories.update({
        _id: success[i]._id
      , "reservations._id": cart._id
    }, {
        $inc: { quantity: success[i].quantity }
      , $pull: { reservations: { _id: cart._id }}
    })
  }

  return
}
```

To rollback we simply pull the reservations out of the `reservations` array.

If we succeeded in reserving all the products we create an order document, set the cart to complete and release all the reservations from the `inventories` collection.

Example 5: Finish up a successful checkout

```
orders.insert({
    created_on: new Date()
  , shipping: {
      name: "Joe Dow"
    , address: "Some street 1, NY 11223"
  }
  , payment: { method: "visa", transaction_id: "2312213312XXXTD" }
  , products: cart.products
});

carts.update({
```

```
12      _id: cart._id, state: 'active'
13    }, {
14      $set: { state: 'completed' }
15    });
16
17    inventories.update({
18      "reservations._id": cart._id
19    }, {
20      $pull: { reservations: { _id: cart._id } }
21    }, false, true);
```

Cleaning up after incomplete checkouts

However, if during the checkout process something happened that ended the checkout process before it finished, we need to clean up the state of the reservations.

Example 6: Cleanup carts

```
1    var cutOffDate = new Date();
2    cutOffDate.setMinutes(cutOffDate.getMinutes() - 30);
3
4    var cartsCol = db.getSisterDB("shop").carts;
5    var productCol = db.getSisterDB("shop").products;
6
7    var carts = cartsCol.find({
8        modifiedOn: { $lte: cutOffDate }, state: 'active'
9      });
10
11   while(carts.hasNext()) {
12     var cart = carts.next();
13
14     for(var i = 0; i < cart.products.length; i++) {
15       var product = cart.products[i];
16
17       productCol.update({
18           _id: product._id
19         , "reservations._id": cart._id
20         , "reservations.quantity": product.quantity
21       }, {
22           $inc: { quantity: product.quantity }
23         , $pull: { reservations: { _id: cart._id }}
```

```
24        });
25      }
26
27      cartsCol.update({
28        _id: cart._id
29      }, {
30        $set: { status: 'expired' }
31      });
32    }
```

To do this, we simply iterate over all the carts and their products and return each of the quantities to the product inventory.

16.4 Indexes

For the carts collection we reference carts by the state field to find expired carts. An index can be added for this field to make the query more efficient.

Example 9: Create the state field index

```
1   var col = db.getSisterDB("catalog").carts;
2   col.ensureIndex({state:1});
```

For the inventories collection, we look up embedded documents in the reservations array by the _id field. We need to create a multi key index for this field.

Example 10: Create the reservations._id field index

```
1   var col = db.getSisterDB("catalog").inventories;
2   col.ensureIndex({"reservations._id":1});
```

For the products and orders collections we do not need any other indexes than the default _id for our examples.

16.5 Scaling

Secondary Reads

All the operations against the cart are write operations so secondary reads are not useful for this schema as they might show out of date carts.

Sharding

Sharding the carts is fairly straight forward as each cart is self-contained. The easiest shard key for this is a hashed _id key as it allows for writing to be distributed as randomly as possible leveraging all the shards.

Example 11: Hashed _id shard key

```
var admin = db.getSisterDB("admin");
db.runCommand({enableSharding:'shop'});
db.runCommand({
    shardCollection: 'shop.carts'
  , key: {_id:'hashed'}
});
```

16.6 Performance

A simple exploration of the performance on a single machine with MongoDb 3.0 shows the difference between MMAP and WiredTiger for a narrow simulation using the schema simulation framework mongodb-schema-simulator.

Scenario

https://github.com/christkv/mongodb-schema-simulator/blob/master/examples/scripts/single_or_replset/cart_no_reservation/cart_5_-item_no_reservation_successful_scenario.js

MongoDb runs locally on a MacBook Pro Retina 2015 with ssd and 16 gb ram. The simulation runs with the following parameters against a single mongodb instance under osx 10.10 Yosemite.

successfully checkout cart parameters

Parameters	
processes	4
poolSize per process	50
type	linear
Resolution in milliseconds	1000
Iterations run	25
Number of products in cart	5
Size of each product in bytes	1024
Number of users	1000
Execution strategy	slicetime

MMAP

The MMAP engine is run using the default settings on MongoDB 3.0.1.

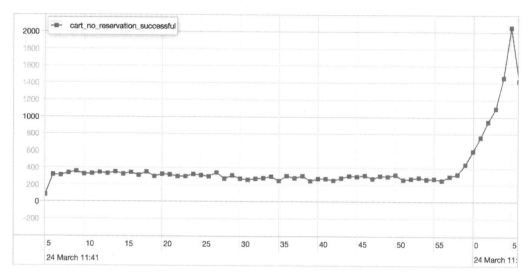

Successfully Checkout Cart

successfully checkout cart

Statistics

Runtime	61.878 seconds
Mean	23696.635 milliseconds
Standard Deviation	12515.697 milliseconds
75 percentile	35072.337 milliseconds
95 percentile	38497.619 milliseconds
99 percentile	40150.439 milliseconds
Minimum	21.637 milliseconds
Maximum	43277.439 milliseconds

WiredTiger

The WiredTiger engine is run using the default settings on MongoDB 3.0.1.

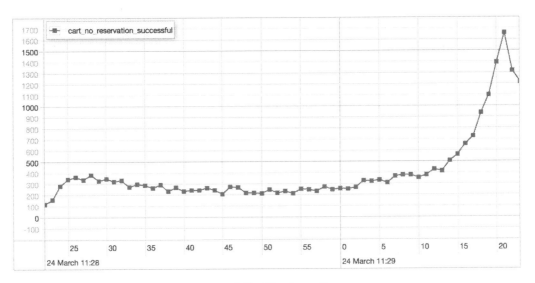

Successfully Checkout Cart

successfully checkout cart

Statistics

Runtime	62.607 seconds
Mean	26075.901 milliseconds
Standard Deviation	12410.047 milliseconds
75 percentile	36122.769 milliseconds
95 percentile	39481.372 milliseconds
99 percentile	41308.47 milliseconds
Minimum	20.228 milliseconds
Maximum	44646.7 milliseconds

This is an `update` heavy schema and this impacts WiredTiger more than `MMAP` due to the need to rewrite the document on each update in `WiredTiger`. Also note that the total runtime is higher than the 25 seconds of load we apply, pointing to the fact that the system is overloaded for this hardware configuration.

16.7 Notes

This seems to be a fairly common pattern for shopping carts now as it simplifies the scaling of the shopping cart by avoiding any inventory validation until the user actually intends to checkout the reserved products. It avoids inventory being locked up in carts that are abandoned.

17. Theater Reservation

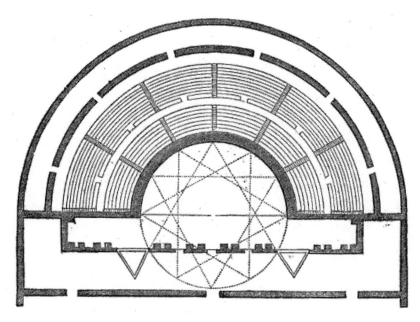

Theater, courtesy of http://en.wikipedia.org/wiki/Roman_theatre_(structure)#/media/File:Plan_Romeins_theater.gif

This schema pattern is based around the concept of buying tickets for a theater. It's a reservation-based schema where the user can pick their own seats and theater session, and the seats are reserved until the user either checks out the cart or the cart expires.

It's a variation of the e-commerce shopping cart for reservations, but has some unique twists to it that makes it a useful pattern to know.

17.1 Schema Observations

- Allows for any type of seated venue layout for reservation.

17.2 Schema

This schema has different components. We have a collection called theaters that contain documents representing theaters. For simplicity's sake, each theater only has a single scene. Below is an example document for the theater The Royal.

```
1   {
2       "_id" : 1
3       , "name" : "The Royal"
4       , "seats" : [ [ 0, 0, 0, 0, 0, 0, 0, 0, 0, 0, 0, 0, 0, 0, 0, 0 ]
5         , [ 0, 0, 0, 0, 0, 0, 0, 0, 0, 0, 0, 0, 0, 0, 0, 0 ]
6         , [ 0, 0, 0, 0, 0, 0, 0, 0, 0, 0, 0, 0, 0, 0, 0, 0 ]
7         , [ 0, 0, 0, 0, 0, 0, 0, 0, 0, 0, 0, 0, 0, 0, 0, 0 ]
8         , [ 0, 0, 0, 0, 0, 0, 0, 0, 0, 0, 0, 0, 0, 0, 0, 0 ] ]
9       , "seatsAvailable" : 80
10  }
```

The schema is fairly straightforward.

Schema Attributes

name	Name of the theater
seats	A 2d array, representing the available seating in the theater
seatsAvailable	The total number of seats in the theater

The most interesting field is the seats field, which contains the map of the theater. It's worth noticing that although we have picked a completely uniform seat layout with the same number of seats in each row, this schema would allow you to create any layout you wish. For example, you could have the following seat layout.

```
1        , "seats" : [
2          , [ 0 ]
3          , [ 0, 0 ]
4          , [ 0, 0, 0 ]
5          , [ 0, 0, 0, 0 ]
6          , [ 0, 0, 0, 0, 0 ] ]
```

Each theater has multiple sessions representing an actual play session. In this schema these are represented by documents in the sessions collection. Below is an example of session for The Royal theater.

```
1     {
2         "_id" : ObjectId("5500632d2dc02be024ba5c66")
3       , "theaterId" : 1
4       , "name" : "Action Movie 5"
5       , "description" : "Another action movie"
6       , "start" : ISODate("2015-03-11T15:45:49.103Z")
7       , "end" : ISODate("2015-03-11T15:45:49.103Z")
8       , "price" : 10
9       , "seatsAvailable" : 80
10      , "seats" : [ [ 0, 0, 0, 0, 0, 0, 0, 0, 0, 0, 0, 0, 0, 0, 0, 0 ]
11        , [ 0, 0, 0, 0, 0, 1, 1, 1, 0, 0, 0, 0, 0, 0, 0, 0 ]
12        , [ 0, 0, 0, 0, 0, 0, 0, 0, 0, 0, 0, 0, 0, 0, 0, 0 ]
13        , [ 0, 0, 0, 0, 0, 0, 0, 0, 0, 0, 0, 0, 0, 0, 0, 0 ]
14        , [ 0, 0, 0, 0, 0, 0, 0, 0, 0, 0, 0, 0, 0, 0, 0, 0 ] ]
15      , "reservations" : [ {
16          "_id": ObjectId("5500632d2dc02be024ba5c66")
17        , "seats": [ [ 1, 5 ], [ 1, 6 ], [ 1, 7 ] ]
18        , "price" : 10
19        , "total" : 30
20      } ]
21    }
```

The schema for a session contains the following fields.

Schema Attributes

theaterId	The Id of the theater the session belongs to
name	The name of the show
description	The description of the show
start	When does the show start
end	When does the show end
price	The price of the show
seatsAvailable	The number of seats left in this session
seats	The 2d array seat map, showing which seats have been booked
reservations	Any current reservations for this session that are in a cart

Notice that the seats field mirrors the seating layout of its parent theater document. In a session, it's used to keep track of what seats have been reserved. The reservations array is an array of current reservations for these sessions before the carts have been checked out.

The shopping cart is fairly straight forward. Let's look at an example cart with a single reservation.

```
1  {
2      "_id" : 1
3      , "state" : "canceled"
4      , "total" : 30
5      , "reservations" : [ {
6          "sessionId" : ObjectId("5500632d2dc02be024ba5c66")
7          , "seats" : [ [ 1, 5 ], [ 1, 6 ], [ 1, 7 ] ]
8          , "price" : 10
9          , "total" : 30
10     } ]
11     , "modifiedOn" : ISODate("2015-03-11T15:45:49.105Z")
12     , "createdOn" : ISODate("2015-03-11T15:45:49.104Z")
13 }
```

The schema for a cart contains the following fields.

Schema Attributes

state	The current state of the cart, one of active, done, canceled or expired
total	The total price of the cart
reservations	An array of reservation documents for sessions. Each document includes the sessionId, the seats reserved, the price per seat and the total for that reservation
modifiedOn	The date the last time the cart was modified
createdOn	The date the cart was created

The most interesting field here is the reservations field, which contains all the current reservations for the cart. Each reservation is for a specific session in a theater.

17.3 Operations

Create a new session

Creating a new session for a specific theater requires us to use the original theater template to create a new session. Let's consider that we have a theater document with _id of 1 and we are creating a new session that will show Action Movie 5.

Example 1: Add a new session

```
1   var theaterId = 1;
2
3   var theaters = db.getSisterDB("booking").theaters;
4   var sessions = db.getSisterDB("booking").sessions;
5
6   var theater = theaters.findOne({"_id": theaterId});
7   sessions.insert({
8       , "name" : "Action Movie 5"
9       , "description" : "Another action movie"
10      , "start" : ISODate("2015-03-11T15:00:00.000Z")
11      , "end" : ISODate("2015-03-11T16:00:00.000Z")
12      , "price" : 10
13      , "seatsAvailable" : theater.seatsAvailable
14      , "seats" : theater.seats
```

```
15      , "reservations" : []
16    });
```

Reserving seats

We are going to reserve some seats for a specific session. To do this, we first need to establish if the session has the desired seats available before adding them to the cart. We are going to reserve the 6th and 7th seats on the 2nd row. (Remember that we are 0 indexed in the arrays and that the first row is the first array) Looking at the seat map for the session, we have marked the seats we are trying to reserve with an X.

```
1  {
2    ...
3    , "seats" : [ [ 0, 0, 0, 0, 0, 0, 0, 0, 0, 0, 0, 0, 0, 0, 0, 0 ]
4      , [ 0, 0, 0, 0, 0, X, X, 0, 0, 0, 0, 0, 0, 0, 0, 0 ]
5      , [ 0, 0, 0, 0, 0, 0, 0, 0, 0, 0, 0, 0, 0, 0, 0, 0 ]
6      , [ 0, 0, 0, 0, 0, 0, 0, 0, 0, 0, 0, 0, 0, 0, 0, 0 ]
7      , [ 0, 0, 0, 0, 0, 0, 0, 0, 0, 0, 0, 0, 0, 0, 0, 0 ] ]
8    ...
9  }
```

Example 2: Reserve seats in a session

```
1   var sessionId = 1;
2   var cartId = 1;
3
4   var seats = [[1, 5], [1, 6]];
5   var seatsQuery = [];
6   var setSeatsSelection = {};
7
8   var sessions = db.getSisterDB("booking").sessions;
9   var session = sessions.find({_id: sessionId});
10
11  for(var i = 0; i < seats.length; i++) {
12    var seatSelector = {};
13    var seatSelection = 'seats.' + seats[i][0] + '.' + seats[i][1];
14    // Part of $and query to check if seat is free
15    seatSelector[seatSelection] = 0;
16    seatsQuery.push(seatSelector);
```

```
17    // Part of $set operation to set seat as occupied
18    setSeatsSelection[seatSelection] = 1;
19  }
20
21  var result = sessions.update({
22        _id: sessionId
23      , $and: seatsQuery
24  }, {
25      $set: setSeatsSelection
26    , $inc: { seatsAvailable: -seats.length }
27    , $push: {
28      reservations: {
29          _id: cartId
30        , seats: seats
31        , price: session.price
32        , total: session.price * seats.length
33      }
34    }
35  });
36
37  // Failed to reserve seats
38  if(result.nModified == 0) ...
39  // Reservation was successful
40  if(result.nModified == 1) ...
```

If the result returns a nModified with the value of 1, we've successfully reserved seats in the session. If nModified equals 0, we could not honor the reservation request (some seats might have been sold out). At this point, an application might choose to retrieve the session document to show the updated view of available seating.

It might look more complicated than previous schemas, but it's fairly straightforward when you break it down. The main thing to remember is that we need to ensure that all seats can be reserved at the same time. To achieve this, we use the $and operator to create an array of all the seats that need to be free in order for the update to be successful. If the selector matches, we need to update all those seats using the $set operator, which that takes a document of key value pairs. The actual update statement we create looks like this.

```
1   sessions.update({
2       _id: 1
3     , $and: [{'seats.1.5': 0}, {'seats.1.6': 0}]
4   }, {
5       $set: {'seats.1.5': 1, 'seats.1.6': 1}
6     , $inc: { seatsAvailable: 2 }
7     , $push: {
8       reservations: {
9           _id: 1
10        , seats: [[1, 5], [1, 6]]
11        , price: 10
12        , total: 20
13      }
14    }
15  });
```

Update cart on successful session reservation

We successfully reserved the seats. Now we need to add those reservations to the shopping cart.

Example 3: Add reservation to the cart

```
1   var sessionId = 1;
2   var cartId = 1;
3
4   var seats = [[1, 5], [1, 6]];
5   var seatsQuery = [];
6   var setSeatsSelection = {};
7
8   var sessions = db.getSisterDB("booking").sessions;
9   var carts = db.getSisterDB("booking").carts;
10  var session = sessions.find({_id: sessionId});
11
12  var result = carts.update({
13      _id: cartId
14    }, {
15      $push: {
16        reservations: {
17            sessionId: sessionId
18          , seats: seats
```

```
19              , price: session.price
20              , total: session.price * seats.length
21          }
22        }
23        , $inc: { total: session.price * seats.length }
24        , $set: { modifiedOn: new Date() }
25    })
26
27  // Failed to add reservation to cart
28  if(result.nModified == 0) ...
29  // Successfully added reservation to cart
30  if(result.nModified == 1) ...
```

As in the previous operation where we tried to reserve seats in a specific session, if nModified equals 1, it means we successfully managed to add the reservation to the cart. If nModified equals 0, we failed to add the reservation (maybe the cart got destroyed). If we failed to add the reservation to the cart, we need to release the reservation on the session document.

Release the seat reservation for a session

To release the reservation, we need to set all the seats we marked with 1 back to 0 for the previously reserved seats.

Example 4: Release all the reservations for a cart

```
1   var sessionId = 1;
2   var cartId = 1;
3
4   var seats = [[1, 5], [1, 6]];
5   var setSeatsSelection = {};
6
7   for(var i = 0; i < seats.length; i++) {
8     setSeatsSelection['seats.' + seats[i][0] + '.' + seats[i][1]] = 0;
9   }
10
11  var sessions = db.getSisterDB("booking").sessions;
12  var result = sessions.update({
13      _id: sessionId
```

```
14    }, {
15        $set: setSeatsSelection
16      , $pull: { reservations: { _id: cartId } }
17    });
18
19  // Failed to release reservation
20  if(result.nModified == 0) ...
21  // Succeded in releasing reservation
22  if(result.nModified == 1) ...
```

To release the reservation we set all the seats in the reservation to 0 and pull the cart reservation from the reservations array in the sessions documents.

Checkout cart

The checkout process consists of a couple of steps. The first one is to create a receipt document in the receipt collection. After creating the receipt, we commit all the reservations on the session before finally setting the cart to done. Let's look at how we create a receipt document.

Example 5: Create receipt

```
1   var cartId = 1;
2
3   var carts = db.getSisterDB("booking").carts;
4   var receipts = db.getSisterDB("booking").receipts;
5
6   var cart = carts.findOne({_id: cartId});
7
8   receipts.insert({
9        createdOn: new Date()
10     , reservations: cart.reservations
11     , total: cart.total
12   });
```

Next, we need to remove all the reservations in the cart from the sessions so as to finalize the reservation of the seats.

Example 6: Commit session reservations

```
1  var cartId = 1;
2
3  var sessions = db.getSisterDB("booking").sessions;
4  session.update({
5      'reservations._id': cartId
6    }, {
7      $pull: { reservations: { _id: id } }
8    }, false, true);
```

This pulls out all the reservations in all sessions where the reservations._id field matches the cartId.

Finally, we mark the cart as done.

Example 7: Mark cart as done

```
1  var cartId = 1;
2
3  var carts = db.getSisterDB("booking").carts;
4  carts.update({
5      _id: cartId
6    }, {
7      $set: { state: 'done' }
8    });
```

Expire carts

If carts are abandoned but contain reservations, we need to release those reservations again so other customers can have the opportunity of reserving them.

Example 8: Expiring shopping carts

```
1   var cutOffDate = new Date();
2   cutOffDate.setMinutes(cutOffDate.getMinutes() - 30);
3
4   var cartsCol = db.getSisterDB("booking").carts;
5   var sessionsCol = db.getSisterDB("booking").sessions;
6
7   var carts = cartsCol.find({
8       modifiedOn: { $lte: cutOffDate }, state: 'active'
9     });
10
11  // Process all carts
12  while(carts.hasNext()) {
13    var cart = carts.next();
14
15    // Process all reservations in the cart
16    for(var i = 0; i < cart.reservations.length; i++) {
17      var reservation = cart.reservations[i];
18      var seats = reservation.seats;
19      var setSeatsSelection = {};
20
21      for(var i = 0; i < seats.length; i++) {
22        setSeatsSelection['seats.' + seats[i][0] + '.' + seats[i][1]] = 0;
23      }
24
25      // Release seats and remove reservation
26      sessionsCol.update({
27        _id: reservation._id
28      }, {
29          $set: setSeatsSelection
30        , $pull: { reservations: { _id: cart._id }}
31      });
32    }
33
34    // Set the cart to expired
35    cartsCol.update({
36      _id: cart._id
37    }, {
38      $set: { status: 'expired' }
39    });
40  }
```

The first step is to retrieve all the expired carts. Next we return all the reservations in the carts to their respective sessions (setting the released seats to 0 in the session documents). Finally we set the cart to the expired state.

This will correctly release any reservations held by timed out shopping carts.

17.4 Indexes

Besides using the _id field to query for carts in the carts collection, we only use the state field for when we are processing expired carts. We should add an index on this field to make the expired carts queries as efficient as possible.

Example 9: Create the state field index

```
var col = db.getSisterDB("booking").carts;
col.ensureIndex({state:1});
```

For the sessions collection we look up sessions by the reservations._id field, so we should add a multikey index for this field.

Example 10: Create the reservations._id field index

```
var col = db.getSisterDB("booking").sessions;
col.ensureIndex({"reservations._id":1});
```

For the theaters and receipts collection we only access documents by the _id field in this example so no additional indexes are needed.

17.5 Scaling

Secondary Reads

All the operations against the cart are write operations so secondary reads are not useful for this schema as they might show out of date carts.

The theaters could be read from secondaries but the sessions should be read from the primary, otherwise they might return an out of date view of the current state of reserved seats.

Sharding

Sharding the carts is fairly straight forward, as each cart is self-contained. The easiest shard key for this is a hashed _id key to allow for writing to be as randomly distributed as possible using all the shards.

Example 11: Hashed _id shard key

```
var admin = db.getSisterDB("admin");
db.runCommand({enableSharding:'booking'});
db.runCommand({
    shardCollection: 'booking.carts'
  , key: {_id:'hashed'}
});
```

You could also shard the theater and sessions as they are self-contained documents. A good key here would be the hashed _id key.

17.6 Performance

A simple exploration of the performance on a single machine with MongoDb 3.0 shows the difference between MMAP and WiredTiger for a narrow simulation using the schema simulation framework mongodb-schema-simulator.

Scenario

https://github.com/christkv/mongodb-schema-simulator/blob/master/examples/scripts/single_or_replset/theater/theater_reserve_-tickets_successfully.js

MongoDb runs locally on a MacBook Pro Retina 2015 with ssd and 16 gb ram. The simulation runs with the following parameters against a single mongodb instance under osx 10.10 Yosemite.

successfully checkout cart parameters

Parameters

processes	4
poolSize per process	50
type	linear
Resolution in milliseconds	1000
Iterations run	25
Number of users	1000
Number of tickets in each cart	5
Execution strategy	slicetime

MMAP

The MMAP engine is run using the default settings on MongoDB 3.0.1.

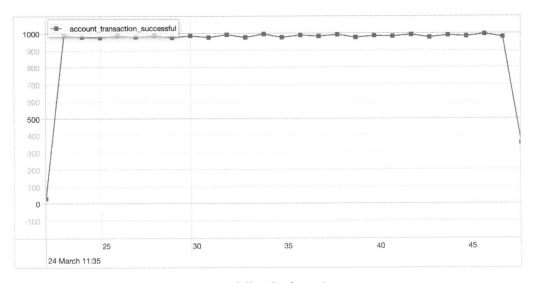

Successfully Checkout Cart

successfully checkout cart

Statistics

Runtime	124.397 seconds
Mean	2292.494 milliseconds
Standard Deviation	1527.972 milliseconds
75 percentile	2916.34 milliseconds
95 percentile	5211.314 milliseconds
99 percentile	7884.857 milliseconds
Minimum	149.741 milliseconds
Maximum	14779.998 milliseconds

WiredTiger

The WiredTiger engine is run using the default settings on MongoDB 3.0.1.

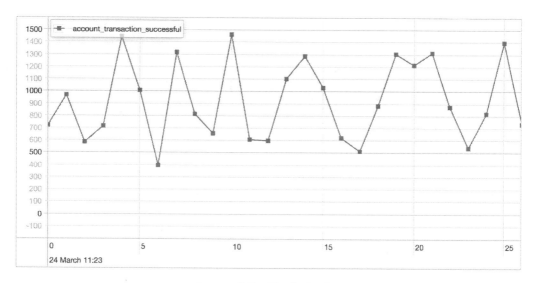

Successfully Checkout Cart

successful cart checkout

Statistics

Runtime	112.994 seconds
Mean	2302.15 milliseconds
Standard Deviation	2052.946 milliseconds
75 percentile	3145.921 milliseconds
95 percentile	6451.251 milliseconds
99 percentile	9608.811 milliseconds
Minimum	19.081 milliseconds
Maximum	17122.854 milliseconds

This is an update heavy schema and this impacts WiredTiger more than MMAP, due to the need to rewrite the full document on each update when using WiredTiger. Also note that the total runtime is higher than the 25 seconds of load we apply, pointing to the fact that the system is overloaded for this hardware configuration.

17.7 Notes

The difference here is sizable between the WiredTiger and MMAP storage engines reflecting the cost of rewriting the documents in WiredTiger due to the lack of in place update support.

18. Account Transactions

Metadata, courtesy of http://www.flickr.com/photos/68751915@N05/6629034769

MongoDB 3.0 support any notion of a transaction across one or more documents. It does, however, guarantee atomic write operations on single documents. This allows us to implement a Two-Phase commit strategy using double bookkeeping to simulate transactions. However, it's important to note that due to only single document operations being atomic, MongoDB can only offer transaction-like semantics. It's still possible for applications to return intermediate results during the two-phase commit or rollback.

In this chapter, we will use two collections to simulate a bank account system. The first collection is **accounts** and contains all the customer accounts, while the second one is **transactions** and is our bookkeeping collection. The goal is to transfer *100* from Joe to Peter using a two-phase commit.

18.1 Schema Observations

- Simple.

- Requires background processes to manage unfinished transactions.
- Can still cause intermediate results during a two-phase commit or rollback.

18.2 Schema

In our simplified schema, we will only keep the basic necessary fields needed to perform the account transaction.

Let's look at an example document representing an account.

```
1  {
2      "_id": ObjectId("54fd7392742abeef6186a68e")
3    , "name": "Joe Moneylender"
4    , "balance": 1000
5    , "pendingTransactions": []
6  }
```

Schema Attributes

name	Name of the account owner (name is used for simplicities sake)
balance	The account balance in a magic universal currency.
pendingTransactions	Contains any pending transactions on the account

A transaction document example would look something like.

```
1  {
2      "_id": ObjectId("54fd7392742abeef6186a68e")
3    , "source": "Joe Moneylender"
4    , "destination": "Peter Bum"
5    , "balance": 200
6    , "state": "initial"
7  }
```

Schema Attributes

source	Name of the source bank account
destination	Name of the destination bank account
balance	Contains the amount of the transaction
state	The state of the transaction. Can be one of `initial`, `pending`, `committed`, `done` and `canceled`

18.3 Operations

Performing a successful Transfer

Create two accounts for Joe and Peter, crediting them each with an initial balance of 1000.

Example 1: Create two accounts

```
var col = db.getSisterDB("bank").accounts;
col.insert({name: "Joe Moneylender", balance: 1000, pendingTransactions:[]});
col.insert({name: "Peter Bum", balance: 1000, pendingTransactions:[]});
```

We are going perform a transfer from Joe to Peter of 100. We start by creating a new transaction and setting its state to initial.

Example 2: Setup initial transaction

```
var col = db.getSisterDB("bank").transactions;
col.insert({source: "Joe", destination: "Peter", amount: 100, state: "intital"});
```

After successfully creating the initial transaction, we are going to attempt to apply it to both accounts. First we need to flip the transaction state to pending in order to signal that we are attempting to apply it to both accounts.

Example 3: Update transaction to pending

```
1  var col = db.getSisterDB("bank").transactions;
2  var transaction = col.findOne({state: "initial"});
3  col.update({_id: transaction._id}, {$set: {state: "pending"}});
```

Next, we attempt to apply the transaction to the source account. The transaction variable represents the previously created transaction document.

Example 4: Debit source account

```
1  var col = db.getSisterDB("bank").accounts;
2  col.update({
3      name: transaction.source, pendingTransactions: {$ne: transaction._id}, balance: {\
4   $gte: amount}
5    }, {
6      $inc: {balance: -transaction.amount}, $push: {pendingTransactions: transaction._i\
7  d}
8    });
```

The update will only succeed if the transaction is not already present on the account and there is enough money to cover the attempted transaction (there is no concept of credit in this world).

If the criteria are met, we push the transaction id to the pendingTransactions embedded array and deduct the amount from the account balance.

After applying the transaction successfully to the source account, we credit the destination account with the transfer amount requested.

Example 5: Credit destination account

```
1   var col = db.getSisterDB("bank").accounts;
2   col.update({
3       name: transaction.source, pendingTransactions: {$ne: transaction._id}, balance: {\
4   $gte: amount}
5     }, {
6       $inc: {balance: -transaction.amount}, $push: {pendingTransactions: transaction._i\
7   d}
8     });
```

As with the source we ensure the transaction does not already exist on the destination account to guard against applying the same transaction multiple times.

Once we have successfully applied the transaction to the source and the destination accounts, our account documents will look something like the following (the pendingTransactions ObjectId entries will vary).

Example 6: Source account

```
1   {
2       "_id": ObjectId("54fd7392742abeef6186a68e")
3     , "name": "Joe Moneylender"
4     , "balance": 900
5     , "pendingTransactions": [ObjectId("54fd7392742abeef6186a68e")]
6   }
```

Example 7: Destination account

```
1   {
2       "_id": ObjectId("54fd7392742abeef6186a68e")
3     , "name": "Joe Moneylender"
4     , "balance": 900
5     , "pendingTransactions": [ObjectId("54fd7392742abeef6186a68e")]
6   }
```

After having applied the transaction to the account, we need to update the transaction state to committed.

Example 8: Update transaction to committed

```
1  var col = db.getSisterDB("bank").transactions;
2  var transaction = col.findOne({state: "pending"});
3  col.update({_id: transaction._id}, {$set: {state: "committed"}});
```

Once the transaction is in committed state, we need to clean up the source and destination accounts by removing the transaction from both accounts. Let's start by removing it from the source account.

Example 9: Remove the transaction from source account

```
1  var col = db.getSisterDB("bank").transactions;
2  col.update({name: transaction.source}, {$pull: {pendingTransactions: transaction._id}\
3  });
```

After removing it from the source account, we remove it from the destination account.

Example 10: Remove the transaction from destination account

```
1  var col = db.getSisterDB("bank").transactions;
2  col.update({name: transaction.source}, {$pull: {pendingTransactions: transaction._id}\
3  });
```

Finally, we set the transaction to the done state, signaling the transfer has been completed.

Example 11: Update transaction to done

```
1  var col = db.getSisterDB("bank").transactions;
2  var transaction = col.findOne({state: "pending"});
3  col.update({_id: transaction._id}, {$set: {state: "done"}});
```

That wraps up the successful transfer of an amount between two accounts. Next, we need to look at potential failure scenarios.

Transaction failure between initial and pending

If there is a failure while flipping the transaction state to pending, the recovery process is to set the transaction state to canceled.

Example 12: Cancel transaction

```
1  var col = db.getSisterDB("bank").transactions;
2  var transaction = col.findOne({state: "initial"});
3  col.update({_id: transaction._id}, {$set: {state: "cancel"}});
```

Transaction failure between pending and committed

We have a partially applied transaction, leaving the transaction in an unfinished state. In this case we need to reverse the transaction.

First reverse the debit of the source account.

Example 13: Reverse debit

```
1  var col = db.getSisterDB("bank").accounts;
2  col.update({
3      name: transaction.source, pendingTransactions: {$in: [transaction._id]}
4    }, {
5      $inc: {balance: transaction.amount}, $pull: {pendingTransactions: transaction._id}
6    });
```

Then, reverse the credit to the destination account.

Example 14: Reverse credit

```
1  var col = db.getSisterDB("bank").accounts;
2  col.update({
3      name: transaction.source, pendingTransactions: {$in: [transaction._id]}
4    }, {
5      $inc: {balance: -transaction.amount}, $pull: {pendingTransactions: transaction._i\
6  d}
7    });
```

Finally, set the transaction itself to the canceled state.

Example 12: Cancel transaction

```
1   var col = db.getSisterDB("bank").transactions;
2   var transaction = col.findOne({state: "initial"});
3   col.update({_id: transaction._id}, {$set: {state: "cancel"}});
```

Transaction failure between committed and done

If the transaction fails between the state of committed and done we need to clean up the state of the accounts.

Example 13: Remove the transaction from source account

```
1   var col = db.getSisterDB("bank").transactions;
2   col.update({name: transaction.source}, {$pull: {pendingTransactions: transaction._id}\
3   });
```

After removing it from the source account remove it from the destination account.

Example 14: Remove the transaction from destination account

```
1   var col = db.getSisterDB("bank").transactions;
2   col.update({name: transaction.source}, {$pull: {pendingTransactions: transaction._id}\
3   });
```

Finally retry changing the transaction state to done.

Recovery Process

It's helpful to have a process running in the background that will look for any transactions left in pending or committed state. To determine the time a transaction has been sitting in an interrupted state, it might be helpful to add a createAt timestamp to all transaction documents.

Undoing/Rolling back a transaction

For some cases you might need to undo (rollback) a transaction due to the application canceling the transaction or because it cannot be recovered (for example, if the one of the accounts does not exist during the transaction).

There are two points in the two-phase commit we can rollback.

1. If you have applied the transaction to the accounts, you should not rollback. Instead, create a new transaction based on the existing transaction and switch the original source and destination fields.
2. If you have created the transaction but have not yet applied it, you can use the following steps.

First set the transaction state to canceling

Example 15: Set transaction state to canceling

```
var col = db.getSisterDB("bank").transactions;
col.update({_id: transaction._id}, {$set: {state: "canceling"}});
```

Next, let's undo the transaction. Notice that a non-applied transaction means the transaction_id has not yet been removed from the pendingTransactions array. Let's undo the transaction on the source account.

Example 16: Undo the source account transaction

```
var col = db.getSisterDB("bank").accounts;
col.update({
    name: transaction.source, pendingTransactions: transaction._id
}, {
    $inc: {balance: transaction.value}, $pull: {pendingTransactions: transaction._id}
});
```

Next undo the transaction on the destination account.

Example 17: Undo the destination account transaction

```
1  var col = db.getSisterDB("bank").accounts;
2  col.update({
3      name: transaction.destination, pendingTransactions: transaction._id
4    }, {
5      $inc: {balance: -transaction.value} , $pull: {pendingTransactions: transaction._i\
6  d}
7    });
```

Finally set the transaction state to canceled

Example 18: Set transaction state to canceled

```
1  var col = db.getSisterDB("bank").transactions;
2  col.update({_id: transaction._id}, {$set: {state: "canceled"}});
```

Concurrent Transaction Application

Let's imagine applications A1 and A2 that both start processing the single transaction, T1 while the transaction is still in the initial' state.

1. A1 can apply T1 before A2 starts
2. A2 will then apply T1 again because it does not appear as pending in the accounts documents.

You can avoid this by explicitly stating in the transaction which application is handling it.

Example 19: Ensuring application isolation

```
1  var col = db.getSisterDB("bank").transactions;
2  col.findAndModify({
3      query: {state: "initial", application: {$exists: 0}}
4    , update: {$set: {state: "pending", application: "A1"}}
5    , new: true});
```

findAndModify will retrieve and update the document in one atomic operation. This guarantees that only a single application can tag a transaction that is being processed by it. In this case, a transaction in the initial state, is marked as being processed by A1 should the application field not exist.

If the transaction fails or needs to be rolled back, you can retrieve the pending transactions for the specific application, A1.

Example 20: Retrieve pending transactions for A1

```
1  var col = db.getSisterDB("bank").transactions;
2  col.transactions.find({application: "A1", state: "pending"});
```

18.4 Indexes

Since we are retrieving transactions by the _id field we do not need any additional indexes for the transactions collection. For the accounts collection we are retrieving the accounts by the name field.

Example 21: Create the bank account name index

```
1  var col = db.getSisterDB("bank").accounts;
2  col.ensureIndex({name:1});
```

If you have processes looking up transactions that are unfinished and are still in the committed or pending states, continuing to either apply the transactions to the accounts or to roll them back, an additional index on the transaction state field will make retrieval of transactions more efficient.

Example 21: Create the transaction account state index

```
1  var col = db.getSisterDB("bank").transactions;
2  col.ensureIndex({state:1});
```

18.5 Scaling

Secondary Reads

All the operations against the queue are write operations so secondary reads are not useful for this schema.

Sharding

In this case we can shard the accounts collection by the name field and use a hashed index for the field to ensure even distribution across all out shards.

Example 22: Shard by accounts name key

```
var admin = db.getSisterDB("admin");
db.runCommand({enableSharding:'bank'});
db.runCommand({
    shardCollection: 'bank.accounts'
  , key: {name:'hashed'}
});
```

For the transactions collection we will hash the _id field as we are looking up transactions mostly by _id. Looking up the transaction by the state field is a rare case that we can let incur a scatter gather query.

Example 23: Shard by transactions _id key

```
var admin = db.getSisterDB("admin");
db.runCommand({enableSharding:'bank'});
db.runCommand({
    shardCollection: 'bank.transactions'
  , key: {_id:'hashed'}
});
```

18.6 Performance

A simple exploration of the performance on a single machine with MongoDb 3.0 shows the difference between MMAP and WiredTiger for a narrow simulation using the schema simulation framework mongodb-schema-simulator.

Scenario

https://github.com/christkv/mongodb-schema-simulator/blob/master/examples/scripts/single_or_replset/account/account_100_-successful_transfer_scenario.js

MongoDb runs on a MacBook Pro Retina 2013 with 512 GB ssd and 16 gb ram. The simulation runs with the following parameters against a single mongodb instance under osx 10.10 Yosemite.

Parameters

processes	4
poolSize per process	50
type	linear
Resolution in milliseconds	1000
Iterations run	25
Number of users querying using metadata per iteration	1000
Execution strategy	slicetime

MMAP

The `MMAP` engine is run using the default settings on `MongoDB 3.0.1`.

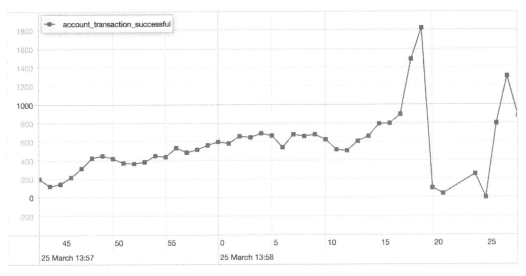

Successfully transfer between accounts

Successfully transfer between accounts

Statistics

Runtime	48.086 seconds
Mean	9951.659 milliseconds
Standard Deviation	7131.847 milliseconds
75 percentile	12220.925 milliseconds
95 percentile	25750.843 milliseconds
99 percentile	34520.997 milliseconds
Minimum	65.398 milliseconds
Maximum	41428.625 milliseconds

WiredTiger

The `WiredTiger` engine is run using the default settings on `MongoDB 3.0.1`.

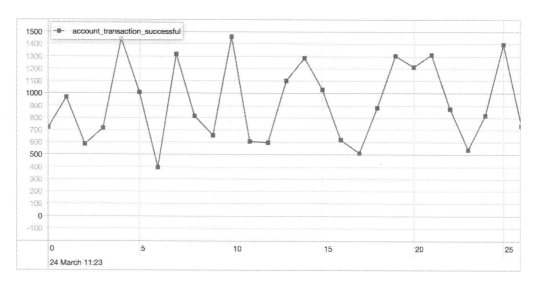

Successfully transfer between accounts

Successfully transfer between accounts

Statistics

Runtime	46.653 seconds
Mean	8655.022 milliseconds
Standard Deviation	5743.181 milliseconds
75 percentile	11037.199 milliseconds
95 percentile	19937.439 milliseconds
99 percentile	29972.029 milliseconds
Minimum	77.812 milliseconds
Maximum	40603.657 milliseconds

The two storage engines MMAP and WiredTiger are fairly close in performance, as the document actually changes are small and thus do not adversely affect WiredTiger performance.

18.7 Notes

 Notes

Real world applications will likely be more complex and require updating more than just the balance of the accounts. The application might need to update pending credits, pending debits and other details.

If these fields are part of the account document they can still occur within a single update, ensuring an atomic update of all the fields.

19. Time Series

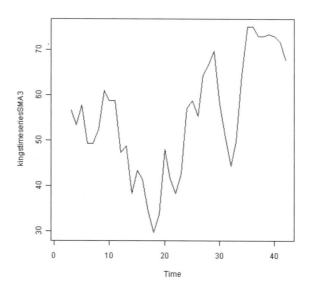

An Example Time Series

A time series is made of discreet measurements at timed intervals. The time series pattern is a write optimization pattern made to ensure maximum write performance throughput for a typical analytics application that stores data in discrete units of time. Examples can include counting the number of page views in a second, or the temperature per minute. For this schema, we will discuss time series in the context of web page views.

19.1 Schema Observations

- The Time series schema is based on efficient, in place updates, which map well to the way the MMAP storage engine works. However, this is not as efficient when using the WiredTiger storage engine due to its lack of in place update support.

19.2 Schema

Schema Attributes	
Optimized For	Write Performance
Preallocation	Benefits from Preallocation on MMAP

To maximize our write throughput for a time series, we are making the assumptions that we€™re interested in discreet buckets of time. That is to say, an individual page view is not attractive to the application by itself. Only the number of page views, in a particular second, minute, hour, day or in a date and time range are of interest. This means the smallest unit of time we want for this example, is a single minute.

Taking that into account, let's model a `bucket` to keep all our page views for a particular minute.

Example 1: A time series bucket

```
{
  "page": "/index.htm",
  "timestamp": ISODate("2014-01-01T10:01:00Z"),
  "totalViews": 0,
  "seconds": {
    "0": 0
  }
}
```

Breaking down the fields.

Field	Description
page	The web page we are measuring
timestamp	The actual minute the bucket is for
totalViews	Total page views in this minute
seconds	Page views for a specific second in the minute

The `bucket` document not only represents the complete number of page views in a particular minute but also contains the breakdown of page views per second inside that minute.

19.3 Operations

Update the Page Views in a Bucket

Let's simulate what happens in an application that is counting page views for a specific page. We are going to simulate updating a bucket, for a specific page view in the 2nd second of the ISODate("2014-01-01T10:01:00Z") bucket.

Example 2: Updating a bucket

```
1    var col = db.getSisterDB("timeseries").pageViews;
2    var secondInMinute = 2;
3    var updateStatment = {$inc: {}};
4    updateStatment["$inc"]["seconds." + secondInMinute] = 1;
5
6    col.update({
7      page: "/index.htm",
8      timestamp: ISODate("2014-01-01T10:01:00Z")
9    }, updateStatment, true)
```

The first part of the updateStatement sets up the $inc value to increment the field in the seconds field named 2, which corresponds with the secondary elapsed second in our bucket time period.

If the field does not exist MongoDB, will set it to one. Otherwise, it will increment the existing value with one. Notice the last parameter of the update statement. This is telling MongoDB to do an upsert which instructs MongoDB to create a new document if none exists that matches the update selector.

Retrieving a specific Bucket

If we wish to retrieve a specific time measurement bucket for a particular minute, we can retrieve it very easily using the timestamp field as shown below.

Example 3: Retrieve a specific bucket

```
1   var col = db.getSisterDB("timeseries").pageViews;
2   pageViews.findOne({
3     page: "/index.htm",
4     timestamp: ISODate("2014-01-01T10:01:00Z")
5   });
```

This will retrieve the bucket for which the `timestamp` matches the time bucket `ISODate("2014-01-01T10:01:00Z")`.

Pre-allocating measurement buckets

To improve performance on writes, we can preallocate buckets to avoid the need to move documents around in memory and on disk. Each bucket document has a known fixed final size. If we use a template to create the empty buckets, we can take advantage of in place updates, minimizing the amount of disk IO needed to collect the page views.

Letâ€™s look at how we can preallocate buckets for a whole hour of measurements. The example function below preAllocateHour, takes a collection, a web page name and a timestamp representing a specific hour.

Example 6: Pre-Allocate buckets for a specific hour

```
1   var preAllocateHour = function(coll, pageName, timestamp) {
2     for(var i = 0; i < 60; i++) {
3       coll.insert({
4         "page": pageName,
5         "timestamp" : timestamp,
6         "seconds" : {
7           "0":0,"1":0,"2":0,"3":0,"4":0,"5":0,"6":0,"7":0,"8":0,"9":0,
8           "10":0,"11":0,"12":0,"13":0,"14":0,"15":0,"16":0,"17":0,"18":0,"19":0,
9           "20":0,"21":0,"22":0,"23":0,"24":0,"25":0,"26":0,"27":0,"28":0,"29":0,
10          "30":0,"31":0,"32":0,"33":0,"34":0,"35":0,"36":0,"37":0,"38":0,"39":0,
11          "40":0,"41":0,"42":0,"43":0,"44":0,"45":0,"46":0,"47":0,"48":0,"49":0,
12          "50":0,"51":0,"52":0,"53":0,"54":0,"55":0,"56":0,"57":0,"58":0,"59":0
13        }
14      })
```

```
15
16      timestamp.setMinutes(timestamp.getMinutes() + 1);
17    }
18 }
```

Let's take this preallocation method out for a test run by preallocating an hour worth of buckets.

Example 7: Call the preAllocate method for a specific hour

```
1 var col = db.getSisterDB("analytics").pageViews;
2 preAllocateHour(col, "index.htm", ISODate("2014-01-01T10:00:00Z"));
```

Let's verify that the preallocation of buckets happened correctly by counting the number of bucket entries generated for the specific hour.

Example 8: Retrieve the number of documents created by the preAllocateHour method

```
1 var col = db.getSisterDB("analytics").pageViews;
2 col.find({timestamp: {$gte: ISODate("2014-01-01T10:00:00Z")},timestamp: {$lt: ISODate\
3 ("2014-01-01T11:00:00Z")} }).count()
```

As we expected the count returned is 60 entries.

19.4 Indexes

Since we will be retrieving the timestamp buckets by their page name and timestamp, the only needed indexes for efficiency are on the page and timestamp fields.

Example 4: Create the timestamp index

```
1 var col = db.getSisterDB("timeseries").pageViews;
2 col.ensureIndex({page:1, timestamp: 1});
```

This will ensure any range queries across the timestamp field will be able to leverage the index for better query performance.

19.5 Scaling

Secondary Reads

Secondary reads might be useful when reporting on the data, as any long running reports on them will cause minimal impact to write throughput.

Sharding

Picking a shard key for a time series will impact the way the data is written and the way it's read.

In the case of the web page analytics example, we wish to summarize the data by page. If the writes for a particular web page are spread out among all the shards, we require scatter/gather queries to correctly summarize data for a specific time period.

We want a shard key that will group all measurements for a specific web page on one specific shard but will spread out the pages across all the shards to maximize write throughput.

We can achieve this by creating a compound shard key which contains the web page name as well as the date.

Example 5: Compound shard key

```
var admin = db.getSisterDB("admin");
db.runCommand({enableSharding:'timeseries'});
db.runCommand({
    shardCollection: 'timeseries.pageViews'
  , key: {page:1, timestamp:1}
});
```

The benefit of using this shard key is that we can still aggregate all the values for a specific page on one shard without forcing a scatter-gather query.

19.6 Performance

A simple exploration of the performance on a single machine with MongoDb 3.0 shows the difference between `MMAP` and `WiredTiger` for a narrow simulation using the schema simulation framework `mongodb-schema-simulator`.

Scenario

https://github.com/christkv/mongodb-schema-simulator/blob/master/examples/scripts/single_or_replset/timeseries/exercise_time_-series.js

MongoDb runs locally on a MacBook Pro Retina 2015 with ssd and 16 gb ram. The simulation runs with the following parameters against a single `mongodb` instance under `osx 10.10 Yosemite`.

Parameters

processes	4
poolSize per process	50
type	linear
Resolution in milliseconds	1000
Iterations run	25
Number of users updating timeseries per iteration	1000
Execution strategy	slicetime

MMAP

The MMAP engine is run using the default settings on MongoDB 3.0.1.

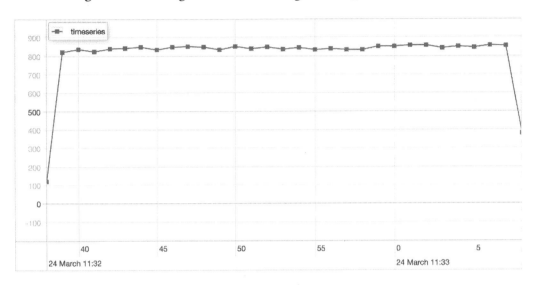

Timeseries Simulation

timeseries scenario results

Statistics

Runtime	30.253 seconds
Mean	1.06 milliseconds
Standard Deviation	1.588 milliseconds
75 percentile	1.246 milliseconds
95 percentile	1.502 milliseconds
99 percentile	1.815 milliseconds
Minimum	0.448 milliseconds
Maximum	57.48 milliseconds

Notice that the 2000 users per second impacts the minimum and maximum as well as the average query time quite a bit.

WiredTiger

The `WiredTiger` engine is run using the default settings on `MongoDB 3.0.1`.

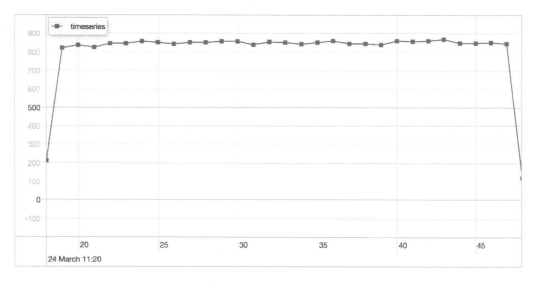

Timeseries Simulation

metadata scenario results

Statistics

Runtime	30.08 seconds
Mean	1.108 milliseconds
Standard Deviation	0.401 milliseconds
75 percentile	1.341 milliseconds
95 percentile	1.871 milliseconds
99 percentile	2.477 milliseconds
Minimum	0.513 milliseconds
Maximum	5.481 milliseconds

As expected there is not much difference between the `MMAP` and `WiredTiger` storage engines when it's a read only workload.

19.7 Notes

Preallocating documents helps MongoDB minimize the document moves in memory, reduce disk IO, and lower fragmentation on disk and in memory. This is especially true for the MMAP storage engine.

20. Array Slice Cache

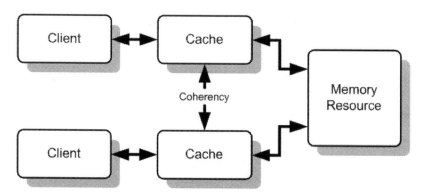

Cache, courtesy of http://upload.wikimedia.org/wikipedia/commons/a/a1/Cache_Coherency_-Generic.png

The array slice cache is a document level cache that leverages the $slice operator in an update statement and allows us to operate on embedded arrays in documents. The operator lets us ensure that an embedded array only has a maximum of n entries in it.

A positive sliceAt will slice from the front and a negative will slice from the end. The first example has a negative sliceAt value. It takes:

```
1  var array = [ 40, 50, 60 ]
2  var sliceAt = -5
3  var items = [ 80, 78, 86 ]
4  var result = [ 50, 60, 80, 78, 86 ]
```

The second example has a positive sliceAt value. It pushes two values to the end of the array and slices it at 3 elements.

```
1  var array = [ 89, 90 ]
2  var sliceAt = 3
3  var items = [ 100, 20 ]
4  var result = [ 89, 90, 100 ]
```

The schema we will showcase here is a blog post document that contains the 10 latest comments inside an embedded array. This embedded array acts as a cache to avoid additional queries against the comments collection when retrieving the main blog web view.

20.1 Schema Observations

- Allows for keeping a cache inside the document itself.
- Lets the application optimize for single document reads.
- Requires additional logic in your application to keep the cache current.

20.2 Schema

In our case, we're are going to use a very simple blog post schema to show how the cache would work.

Let's look at a post document from the posts collection with a single comment.

```
1  {
2      "_id": ObjectId("54fd7392742abeef6186a68e")
3    , "blogId": ObjectId("54fd7392742abeef6186a68e")
4    , "createdOn": ISODate("2015-03-11T12:03:42.615Z")
5    , "publishedOn": ISODate("2015-03-11T12:03:42.615Z")
6    , "title": "Awesome blog post"
7    , "content": "Testing this blog software"
8    , "latestComments": [{
9          "_id": ObjectId("54fd7392742abeef6186a68e")
10        , "publishedOn": ISODate("2015-03-11T12:03:42.615Z")
11        , "message": "Awesome post"
12     }]
13 }
```

A simple comment document from the comments collection.

```
1  {
2      "_id": ObjectId("54fd7392742abeef6186a68e")
3    , "postId": ObjectId("54fd7392742abeef6186a68e")
4    , "publishedOn": ISODate("2015-03-11T12:03:42.615Z")
5    , "message": "Awesome post"
6  }
```

20.3 Operations

Add a comment

When a user enters a comment, it first gets written into the comments collection and then added to the latestComments embedded array cache in the blog post document. For this example, we are going assume, that we have a blog post in the posts collection with the field _id set to the value 1.

Example 1: Add comment to the latestComments cache

```
1  var postId = 1;
2  var posts = db.getSisterDB("blog").posts;
3  var comments = db.getSisterDB("blog").comments;
4
5  var comment = {
6      "_id": ObjectId("54fd7392742abeef6186a68e")
7    , "postId": postId
8    , "publishedOn": ISODate("2015-03-11T12:03:42.615Z")
9    , "message": "Awesome post"
10 };
11
12 comments.insert(comment);
13
14 posts.update({
15     "_id": postId
16   }, {
17     latestComments: {
18         $each: [comment]
19       , $slice: -10
20     }
21   });
```

This will add the new comment to the end of the `latestComments` embedded array and slice it from the start at 10 elements. To display the ten latest comments in descending order, all we would need to do is read the blog post document and reverse the `latestComments` array to get the comments in the right order.

20.4 Indexes

We do not need any specific indexes in this example as we are always referencing documents by the `_id` field.

20.5 Scaling

Secondary Reads

The secondary reads will come with a latency penalty given that any changes to the cache might take some time to replicate across to the secondaries. However, depending on the applications' needs, this latency might be acceptable. An example might be a Content Management System (CMS) where publishing an article might not need to be immediately available across the entire web site.

Here, secondary reads would allow us to offload reads from the primary, and distribute the load across multiple secondaries.

Sharding

For sharding it makes sense to select a shard key that places all blog posts on the same shard. For the comments you also want all the comment queries to be routed to the same shard for a specific blog post.

To do this efficiently, we should use a compound shard key that will contain a routing part (the blogId) as well as a rough time stamp (ObjectId). In our case, the logical key is `{blogId: 1, _id: 1}` for the `posts` collection.

Example 2: Sharding key posts collection

```
var admin = db.getSisterDB("admin");
db.runCommand({enableSharding:'blogs'});
db.runCommand({
    shardCollection: 'blogs.posts'
  , key: {blogId:1, _id:1}
});
```

Similarly for the comments collection we should group the comments together on the same shard so we can create a compound shard key {postId:1, _id:1} routing by postId.

Example 2: Sharding key comments collection

```
var admin = db.getSisterDB("admin");
db.runCommand({enableSharding:'blogs'});
db.runCommand({
    shardCollection: 'blogs.comments'
  , key: {postId:1, _id:1}
});
```

20.6 Performance

Performance is good here as the $slice update operator ensures we do mostly in place updates. In the case of the blog example, we might get more document moves as the size of latestComments might change due to different comment sizes. In cases where we use uniform sized documents, we will not incur any additional document moves.

> T Preallocate T T If we have uniform sized documents to be inserted into the document level line cache we can avoid document moves by pre-allocating the embedded document by filling it with empty documents of the expected size, meaning the document will not be moved around once we start pushing documents into the cache.

A simple exploration of the performance on a single machine with MongoDb 3.0 shows the difference between MMAP and WiredTiger for a narrow simulation using the schema simulation framework mongodb-schema-simulator.

Scenario

https://github.com/christkv/mongodb-schema-
simulator/blob/master/examples/scripts/single_or_replset/array_slice/cache_slice_-
scenario.js
https://github.com/christkv/mongodb-schema-
simulator/blob/master/examples/scripts/single_or_replset/array_slice/pre_allocated_-
cache_slice_scenario.js

MongoDb runs locally on a MacBook Pro Retina 2015 with ssd and 16 gb ram. The simulation runs with the following parameters against a single `mongodb` instance under `osx 10.10 Yosemite`.

Pre-allocated slice cache

Parameters

processes	4
poolSize per process	50
type	linear
Resolution in milliseconds	1000
Iterations run	25
Number of users	1000
Execution strategy	slicetime

Slice cache no pre-allocation

Parameters

processes	4
poolSize per process	50
type	linear
Resolution in milliseconds	1000
Iterations run	25
Number of users	1000
Execution strategy	slicetime

MMAP

The MMAP engine is run using the default settings on MongoDB 3.0.1.

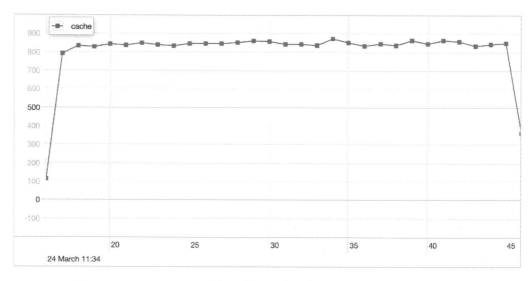

Pre-allocated cache

Pre-allocated slice cache

Statistics

Runtime	30.98 seconds
Mean	0.668 milliseconds
Standard Deviation	0.163 milliseconds
75 percentile	0.715 milliseconds
95 percentile	0.874 milliseconds
99 percentile	1.155 milliseconds
Minimum	0.361 milliseconds
Maximum	5.799 milliseconds

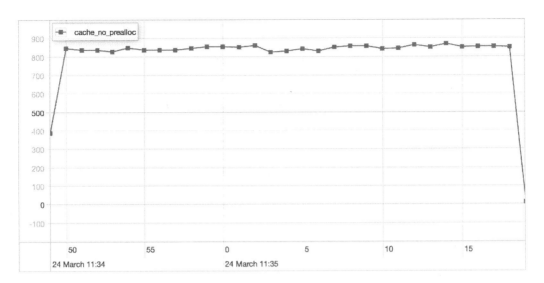

Slice cache no pre-allocation

Slice cache no pre-allocation

Statistics

Runtime	30.507 seconds
Mean	0.663 milliseconds
Standard Deviation	0.155 milliseconds
75 percentile	0.715 milliseconds
95 percentile	0.86 milliseconds
99 percentile	1.088 milliseconds
Minimum	0.365 milliseconds
Maximum	8.494 milliseconds

WiredTiger

The `WiredTiger` engine is run using the default settings on `MongoDB 3.0.1`.

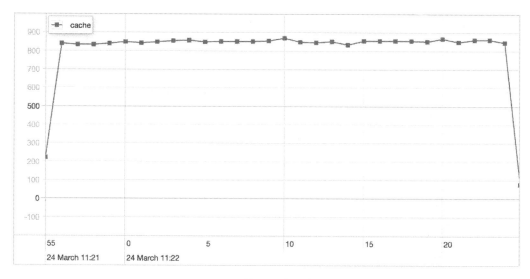

Pre-allocated cache

Pre-allocated slice cache

Statistics

Runtime	30.606 seconds
Mean	0.756 milliseconds
Standard Deviation	0.199 milliseconds
75 percentile	0.812 milliseconds
95 percentile	1.085 milliseconds
99 percentile	1.418 milliseconds
Minimum	0.408 milliseconds
Maximum	5.627 milliseconds

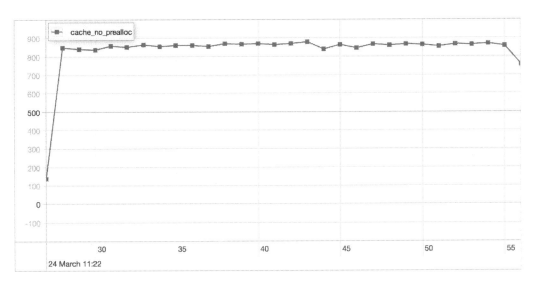

Slice cache no pre-allocation

Slice cache no pre-allocation

Statistics

Runtime	30.033 seconds
Mean	1.012 milliseconds
Standard Deviation	0.4 milliseconds
75 percentile	1.234 milliseconds
95 percentile	1.783 milliseconds
99 percentile	2.185 milliseconds
Minimum	0.417 milliseconds
Maximum	8.582 milliseconds

The variance between MMAP and WiredTiger is minor in both cases. The small difference between pre-allocation and no pre-allocation is mostly due to the fact that we have a uniform object size in this test. If the cache document size is fairly big, it will impact WiredTiger since it needs to rewrite more data on each update.

20.7 Notes

This is an effective way cache results in the main document without incurring the side effects of unbound growing embedded documents. It's a strategy that is useful when you wish to optimize for single document reads for specific web or application views. In this specific example, we can imagine a web page view showing a blog post with its ten latest comments.

21. Internationalization

Earth, courtesy of http://upload.wikimedia.org/wikipedia/commons/2/22/Earth_Western_-Hemisphere_transparent_background.png

In this internationalization example, we show a schema that might be useful for when you have to support multiple languages on an international site. We are going to use products and product categories in our example. This is a very simplified example and does not take into consideration more esoteric edge cases of i18 support.

21.1 Schema Observations

- Allow for single document reads, including all the translation information for efficient multi language support.
- The need to perform potentially mass updates can be costly if the translations are frequently changing.

21.2 Schema

Below is an example category document. The field `names` is an embedded document keyed by the language. In this case `en-us` means `american english` and the name of the category is `car`.

```
1  {
2    "_id" : 1
3    , "names" : {
4      "en-us" : "car"
5    }
6  }
```

The product contains all the categories as well, so that we can easily show the right name depending on the users preferred language. This is to optimize for single document retrieval avoid multiple round trips to the database. We will look at the trade off we make for this optimization later.

```
1  {
2      "_id" : 1
3    , "name" : "car"
4    , "cost" : 100
5    , "currency" : "usd"
6    , "categories" : [{
7        "_id" : 1
8        , "names" : { "en-us" : "car" }
9    } ]
10   }
```

21.3 Operations

Add a new translation to a category

We are going to add the `de-de` local to the `car` category shown above. For simplicity's sake we will assume this category is identified by the `_id` field set to the value `1`.

Example 1: Add a new translation

```
1   var categoryId = 1;
2
3   var categories = db.getSisterDB("shop").categories;
4   var products = db.getSisterDB("shop").products;
5
6   categories.update({
7       _id: categoryId
8     }, {
9       $set: {
10          "categories.$.names.de-de": 'auto'
11      }
12    });
13
14  products.update({
15      "categories._id": categoryId
16    }, {
17      $set: {
18          "categories.$.names.de-de": 'auto'
19      }
20    })
```

In the first step, we update the category by adding the new de-de local to the document.

In the second step, we need to update all the caches of all documents that contain the car category. The update statement looks for all products where the categoires._id field matches categoryId. Then, on the first matching document for that categoryId, it adds the new local.

Removing a translation from a category

If we wish to remove a translation from a category, we need to first remove it from the category and then update all the product caches.

Example 1: Remove a translation

```
1   var categoryId = 1;
2
3   var categories = db.getSisterDB("shop").categories;
4   var products = db.getSisterDB("shop").products;
5
6   categories.update({
7       _id: categoryId
8   }, {
9       $unset: {
10          "categories.$.names.de-de": 'auto'
11      }
12  });
13
14  products.update({
15      "categories._id": categoryId
16  }, {
17      $unset: {
18          "categories.$.names.de-de": 'auto'
19      }
20  })
```

Just as when adding it, the only change is that we are using the $unset update operator to remove the field from the embedded documents.

21.4 Indexes

In this example there are special indexes used other than the _id index.

21.5 Scaling

Secondary Reads

If the site is read heavy (say a product catalog), it might make sense to offload reads to secondary servers to scale reading. It comes down to the application's acceptable latency level as there might be some delay between a write happening on a primary until it's been replicated across to the secondary.

Sharding

The multi language pattern does not really benefit from sharding. It's more likely that you would shard the collections based on other criteria.

21.6 Performance

There is a very obvious trade off being made here. We are exchanging the costs of updating all the products each time we add or remove a local against the need to perform multiple reads on the `categories` collection. Since adding new translations are not likely to happen constantly, the added updates to the `products` collection are insignificant against the benefit of performing single document reads when retrieving the product documents.

A simple exploration of the performance on a single machine with MongoDb 3.0 shows the difference between `MMAP` and `WiredTiger` for a narrow simulation using the schema simulation framework `mongodb-schema-simulator`.

Scenario
https://github.com/christkv/mongodb-schema-simulator/blob/master/examples/scripts/single_or_-replset/multilanguage/multilanguage_add_new_local_scenario.js https://github.com/christkv/mongodb-schema-simulator/blob/master/examples/scripts/single_or_-replset/multilanguage/multilanguage_remove_local_scenario.js

MongoDb runs locally on a MacBook Pro Retina 2015 with ssd and 16 gb ram. The simulation runs with the following parameters against a single `mongodb` instance under `osx 10.10 Yosemite`.

Add a local to a category

Parameters

processes	4
poolSize per process	50
type	linear
Resolution in milliseconds	1000
Iterations run	25
Number of users adding locals to category iteration	1000
Execution strategy	slicetime

Remove a local from a category

Parameters

processes	4
poolSize per process	50
type	linear
Resolution in milliseconds	1000
Iterations run	25
Number of users adding locals to category iteration	1000
Execution strategy	slicetime

MMAP

The MMAP engine is run using the default settings on MongoDB 3.0.1.

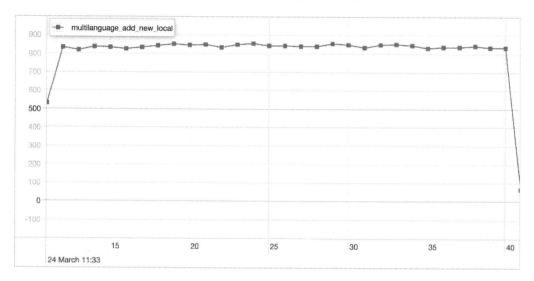

Add Local to Category Simulation

add local to category scenario results

Statistics

Runtime	30.898 seconds
Mean	0.676 milliseconds
Standard Deviation	0.202 milliseconds
75 percentile	0.716 milliseconds
95 percentile	0.865 milliseconds
99 percentile	1.446 milliseconds
Minimum	0.391 milliseconds
Maximum	6.839 milliseconds

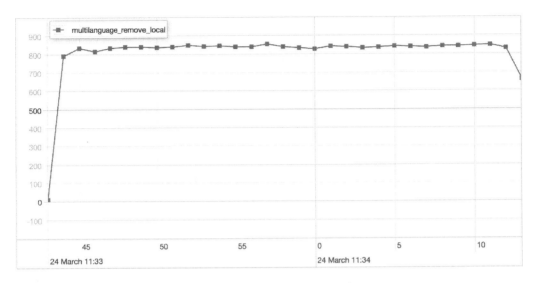

Remove Local from Category Simulation

remove local from category scenario results

Statistics

Runtime	31.037 seconds
Mean	0.675 milliseconds
Standard Deviation	0.185 milliseconds
75 percentile	0.715 milliseconds
95 percentile	0.867 milliseconds
99 percentile	1.418 milliseconds
Minimum	0.403 milliseconds
Maximum	5.882 milliseconds

As expected the performance is similar because the patterns are similar. We would expect the performance to be tied to the amount of documents that need to be updated when a new local is added to a category.

WiredTiger

The `WiredTiger` engine is run using the default settings on `MongoDB 3.0.1`.

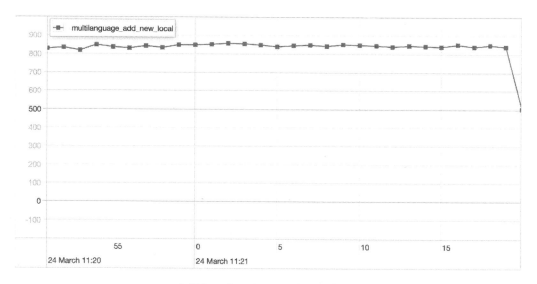

Add Local to Category Simulation

add local to category scenario results

Statistics

Runtime	30.681 seconds
Mean	0.693 milliseconds
Standard Deviation	0.219 milliseconds
75 percentile	0.73 milliseconds
95 percentile	0.889 milliseconds
99 percentile	1.582 milliseconds
Minimum	0.409 milliseconds
Maximum	7.157 milliseconds

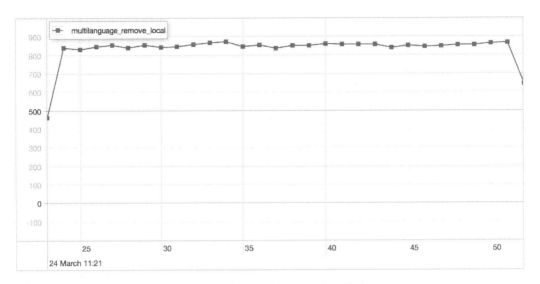

Remove Local from Category Simulation

remove local from category scenario results

Statistics

Runtime	30.404 seconds
Mean	0.913 milliseconds
Standard Deviation	0.337 milliseconds
75 percentile	1.145 milliseconds
95 percentile	1.316 milliseconds
99 percentile	1.763 milliseconds
Minimum	0.409 milliseconds
Maximum	7.938 milliseconds

WiredTiger is a bit slower than MMAP for this schema as it involves a lot of in place updates that causes the storage engine to rewrite the entire document.

21.7 Notes

It's important to consider the trade off of caching vs performing multiple queries. In this case it's pretty obvious the caching strategy will pay off but there might be situations where it doesn't.

Let's say you are caching stock ticker prices in a portfolio object where the stock ticker is constantly changing. The constant changes and required writes will offset any benefit of caching the latest stock prices in the portfolio document. In this case, it's better to fetch the latest stock prices from a the `prices` collections instead.

High rate of change

One more thing to consider is that if you find your application is constantly adding new categories or translations it might be beneficial to duplicate the product information making an identical document for each language allowing for single document reads for any language and avoiding massive updates across all possible products.

49754631R00124

Made in the USA
Middletown, DE
22 October 2017